INTERNATIONAL JOURNAL OF
BEHAVIORAL MEDICINE

Volume 12, Number 2   2005

Special Issue
on
Positive Psychology in Behavioral Medicine

International Journal of Behavioral Medicine
2005, Vol. 12, No. 2, 47–49

An Exploration of the Health Benefits of Factors
That Help Us to Thrive

Positive psychology has come of age. Interest is shifting beyond stress, depression, and other psychosocial factors that limit health and functioning toward the exploration of human strengths and factors that allow us to flourish and the ways they promote health and functioning. What are these human strengths? What are the social and environmental factors that allow us to flourish and thrive? Historically, this research focused on social support as the main factor that promotes health and functioning. However, with increasing interest in positive psychology comes a broadening of the range of factors to be considered. It is our aim in this special issue of the International Journal of Behavioral Medicine to feature some of these new factors and to highlight research that is ongoing, or is needed, to identify links to physical health and pathways by which these links may occur. To do this, we have included three review articles—a general overview of the field, a review of research on oxytocin that is a potentially important physiologic mechanism, and a review of research on altruism that highlights the benefits of helping as a contrast to the more extensively studied benefits of being helped. The empirical articles focus on the health benefits of such diverse factors as life meaning, optimism, sense of coherence, and pet ownership. The issue concludes with an examination of how people recover from depression.

The Chesney, Darbes, Hoerster, Taylor, and Chambers article is a comprehensive review that identifies the most promising emerging evidence on the impact of positive psychological states on physiology, health behaviors, and social conditions. Intriguing evidence is provided for a variety of physiological systems that can be influenced by positive emotional states. A particularly important focus of this review is on the impact of interventions, such as coping effectiveness training or meditation, which can increase positive emotional states.

A more detailed examination of one potentially important physiological pathway by which positive emotional states get into the body is presented in the Uvnäs-Moberg and Magnusson article. It is of interest that we know considerably more about the physiological pathways that link negative psychosocial factors and health than we do about the positive physiological links. It makes sense that because the brain is well integrated to respond to stress, it similarly may have one or more systems in place to foster calm and connection

responses. One of these systems is the brain peptide oxytocinergic system, potentially induced by touch and warmth and acting in contrast to the fight-or-flight response to stress. These researchers have conducted seminal work in this area. In their review, they not only present a range of physiological and neurological evidence to support the importance of the oxytocinergic system but they also highlight their own work. It is exciting to see how the thinking of these leaders in the field has evolved and what they currently see as the challenges to understanding the effects of the oxytocinergic system on the central nervous system.

When one offers help to another, who benefits? In the past, we have focused on the one who is helped. But what about the helper? The Post article reviews existing data on the health benefits of altruism and includes not only empirical research but work from evolutionary biology and the humanities. He begin with a paradox. Although we have more material wealth now than we have had in past generations, we are not happier. Most religions argue that materialism does not bring happiness. If this is true, it begs the question of what does bring happiness. Most religions advocate the practice of serving, most frequently in the form of volunteerism. The Post article suggests that this is one pathway to happiness, well-being, health, and longevity. However, considerably more research is needed in this area. We need to develop good instruments that measure the act of helping and also include questions about the extent to which the helper is overburdened by the helping role. Potential public health benefits not only for the individual but also for society are significant.

Our first empirical article, by Skrabski, Kopp, Rozsa, Rethelyi, and Rahe, focuses on the connection between life meaning and health in Hungary. The problem in Eastern Europe is that premature mortality is on the rise, in contrast to the clear decline observed in Western Europe. To understand the reasons for this and, ultimately, to identify ways to intervene, Hungarostudy 2002 was developed as a cross-sectional survey of 12,640 people, drawn from 150 subregions representative of the Hungarian population. The authors argue that new approaches are needed to understand the health deterioration that occurs in societies in transition. Their hypothesis is that loss of life meaning has adverse implications for mortality, as well as for physical health, disability, and mental health. A particularly interesting aspect of this article is the combination of individual analyses of life meaning and self-reported health in their large sample of more than 12,000 people and ecological analyses linking life meaning to regional mortality rates.

The second empirical article, by Ironson et al., examines another construct central to the field of positive psychology, namely optimism. It poses two fundamental questions: does optimism slow progression of a serious illness and, if so, how? The illness providing the backdrop for this longitudinal study is HIV. This is clearly a devastating illness but also one that has become manageable with medications and the appropriate mindset. The authors argue that optimism is this salutary mindset and that those who are optimistic have a slower progression of HIV over 2 years. A particularly nice feature of this article is that they take the next step and identify three key pathways by which optimism influences progression: a behavioral pathway (more proactive behavior), a cognitive pathway (less avoidant coping), and an affective pathway (less depression). They conclude with a discussion of how to intervene on optimism and thus influence its respective mediator pathways.

Lindfors, Lundberg, and Lundberg focus on an old positive psychology construct and link it to important biomarkers of cardiovascular health. Sense of coherence, developed by Antonovsky in the 1980s, is a global life orientation consisting of three related dimensions—comprehensibility (knowing how to deal with something), manageability (being able to deal with it), and meaningfulness (being able to grasp the meaning of the actions taken). All three of these dimensions are needed to cope well with everyday stressors and maximize health. Those with a low sense of coherence view life as unorganized and meaningless and view themselves as lacking in the resources needed to deal with it. In a representative sample of 244 nonsmoking, premenopausal women, the authors find a link between a brief, three-item measure of coherence and levels of blood pressure and cholesterol, after adjusting for other cardiovascular risk factors. Intuitively, this concept makes good sense as a potentially important buffer against everyday stressors. The ease with which it can be measured encourages further exploration in large datasets that include a range of both standard and psychosocial risk factors. Such further exploration will determine the extent to which, and how, sense of coherence acts as an independent biological buffer against ill health and disease.

Connections with others are important to health. In the past, we have focused on *social* connections. However, pet ownership is another type of connection that is characteristic of the lives of between 30% to 40% of the population. There is a growing literature on the health benefits of pet ownership, mediated by such mechanisms as stress reduction, increased physical activity, and meaningful social activity. Pachana, Ford, Andrew, and Dobson examine the association between pet ownership and self-reported physical and mental health in a large sample of elderly Australian women. Although the findings are equivocal, it is clear that the study of animal–human relationships must deal adequately with confounders, particularly socioeconomic factors, which influence both ownership and health. As in any type of relationship, pet ownership is likely to have both positive and negative implications. It is time to take the next step in this research and develop focused measures that get beyond the existence of pets in the household and assess the importance of these pets to the household. Moreover, creative ways to use randomized designs that will provide the best control for confounders are needed.

This special issue would not be complete if we did not devote some attention to promising interventions. The Hayes, Beevers, Feldman, Laurenceau, and Perlman article describes a newly developed intervention to help people recover from depression. Depression is a leading cause of disability that adversely affects such medical illnesses as cardiovascular disease, cancer, HIV and AIDS, and diabetes. Although a number of treatments for depression exist, their efficacy ranges 50% to 60% and they have disturbingly high relapse rates. This new psychotherapy not only aims to reduce the depression by targeting avoidance and rumination but also seeks to build skills to foster hope, healthy views of the self, and healthy lifestyle behaviors. Although this intervention was conducted on only 29 participants, the efficacy data are promising in that depression improved significantly and was related to more active processing of negative emotions and less avoidance of them.

In summary, this special issue of the *International Journal of Behavioral Medicine* provides a sampling of the range of topics that are under investigation in the emerging field of positive psychology. Psychological, social, and spiritual factors are likely to foster human strengths and help people thrive. Biochemical, affective, cognitive, and behavioral links among these factors and important physical health outcomes are apparent. Some of the methodological challenges to, and opportunities for, the conduct of rigorous research in this area have been identified. There is a need for interventions that aim to promote human strengths but very few currently exist. We hope that this special issue will help to move this field forward by helping readers to formulate new questions and foster new research. We are glad to be a part of this endeavor.

Gail H. Ironson
Lynda H. Powell

We would also like to thank two people who were an enormous help to us in making this issue possible. Dr. Heidemarie Kremer, the key administrative colleague for Dr. Ironson, and Michelle Wayman, the key administrative colleague for Dr. Powell. Reviewers who helped the editors make decisions about the articles and whose comments helped to make this issue immeasurably better are the following:

Karen Allen
Stephanie Brown
Erin Costanzo
Ron Duran
Michael Friedman
Melissa Hunt
Thomas F. Garrity
Dale Ironson
Raija Kalimo
Jaakko Kaprio
Stanislav Kasl
Cheryl Koopman
Heidemarie Kremer
Jane Leserman
Kathleen Light

William Lovallo
Judy Luborsky
Mark Lumley
Susan K. Lutgendorf
Nancy McCain
Judith Moskowitz
Douglas Oman
Marcia Ory
Deidre Pereira
Carol Ryff
Carolyn Schwartz
Suzanne Segerstrom
Howard Tennen
Antti Uutela
Karen Wyche

International Journal of Behavioral Medicine
2005, Vol. 12, No. 2, 50–58

Positive Emotions: Exploring the Other Hemisphere in Behavioral Medicine

Margaret A. Chesney, Lynae A. Darbes, Kate Hoerster, Jonelle M. Taylor,
Donald B. Chambers, David E. Anderson

The search for the psychological antecedents of medical disorders has focused on the role of stress and negative emotional states. Previous research in this area has investigated relations between negative emotions and physiological adaptations (e.g., blood pressure elevations), adverse health behaviors (e.g., smoking), and social conditions (e.g., social isolation). In this discussion, we argue that more attention is needed to understand the effects of positive emotional states on health enhancement and disease prevention. In each of the areas cited previously, evidence is beginning to emerge that indicates that positive emotions can be associated with health promoting conditions. Interventions using cognitive behavioral strategies or meditation can increase positive emotional states that are maintained over time and that may benefit health and well-being. Implications for behavioral medicine are discussed.

Key words: positive affect, emotion, health, behavioral medicine

Historically, medicine evolved as a search for methods to alleviate or eliminate disease in the individual patient. From the earliest attempts to repel evil spirits by shamans with their rituals and potions (Frank, 1961) to the modern emphasis on molecular malfunction and pharmacological intervention, the focus has been on pathology, that is, on the negative. In ancient times, for example, many diseases were thought to result from negative emotions that produced imbalances in bodily fluids. This mind–body orientation to understanding disease prevailed throughout Europe until the Renais-

Margaret A. Chesney, Lynae A. Darbes, Kate Hoerster, Jonelle M. Taylor, Donald B. Chambers, all at the Department of Medicine, University of California–San Francisco, San Francisco, CA, USA; David E. Anderson, National Institute on Aging, National Institutes of Health, Bethesda, MD, USA.

Margaret A. Chesney is now at the National Center of Complementary and Alternative Medicine, National Institutes of Health.

This article is based on a presentation given by the first author at the International Congress of Behavioral Medicine, Helsinki, Finland, August 2002.

This work was supported by grants R01 MH57233 (Margaret A. Chesney, principal investigator) and P30-MH62246 (Thomas J. Coates, principal investigator) from the National Institute of Mental Health. The authors thank Susan Folkman and Judith Moskowitz at the Osher Center for Integrative Medicine at the University of California, San Francisco, for their collaboration and guidance in the theoretical aspects of enhancing positive affect and meaning through coping effectiveness training (CET). We also thank the dedicated staff members and participants of the CET research trials.

Correspondence concerning this article should be addressed to Margaret A. Chesney, Deputy Director, National Center for Complementary and Alternative Medicine, National Institutes of Health, 31 Center Drive, Room 2B11, MSC 2182, Bethesda, Maryland 20892–2182. E-mail: chesneym@mail.nih.gov

sance, when an empirical approach to medical science developed in a philosophical milieu that considered the mind and body as belonging to separate realms (Gorham, 1994). Thereafter, medical science turned to a study of anatomy and physiology that had little place for mind–body interactions.

Clinical practitioners continued to notice, however, that the emotions and attitudes of their patients could play an important role in health outcomes. For example, Sir William Osler observed, more than a century ago, that "it is much more important to know what sort of a patient has the disease than what sort of disease a patient has" (Silverman, Murray, & Brian, 2003, p. 43). Modern behavioral medicine evolved following a series of landmark developments that emphasized stress and negative emotional states, including repressed emotions. Franz Alexander (1939) postulated, for example, that unconscious emotional conflicts potentiate chronic conditions, such as hypertension, via sustained disturbances of autonomic nervous system activity. Over the same period, the concept of "psychological stress" was introduced to describe environmentally induced disruptions in homeostatic mechanisms, notably in the sympathetic nervous and adrenocortical systems, which were thought to decrease resistance to disease (Cannon, 1929; Selye, 1956). More recently, the "biopsychosocial" model was proposed with its emphasis on "conservation-withdrawal" as a protective response to stress (Engel, 1971). The observation of the Type A behavior pattern (Rosenman et al., 1975) in patients with coronary artery disease led to a search for its pathogenic components by behavioral medicine researchers. Anger and hostility (and more recently, depression) emerged as a focus of attention in the search for the emotional antecedents of cardiovascular disease (Bush et al., 2001).

In this article, we add our voices to those who have argued that the positive "hemisphere" in the global world of emotional life is worthy of increased experimental attention in the search for methods to enhance health and prevent disease (Salovey, Rothman, Detweiler, & Steward, 2000; Taylor, Kemeny, Reed, Bower, & Gruenewald, 2000). We cite studies of the effects of negative emotions that have been conducted in three primary domains: those of physiological adaptations to stress, maladaptive behaviors, and social environments. We assert that positive emotions are associated with health-inducing effects that are not necessarily the same as those associated with the absence of negative emotions. We review evidence that suggests that positive and negative emotions may not be mutually exclusive. Recent evidence from each of these domains of research—physiology, behavior, and social environment—is cited in support of this argument. Most previous behavioral interventions have been applied to reduce stress and alleviate negative emotional states. Although less attention has focused on interventions to increase positive emotional states, we propose that such interventions should receive more attention because of their possible salutary effects on health. We conclude with a description of recent clinical interventions in which the effects of experimentally induced positive emotional states on health benefits were observed.

Negative Emotional States and Adverse Health Outcomes

Most previous studies on negative emotional states in disease pathogenesis and progression have focused largely on two emotional states, anger and depression. Anger arises in response to situations that are perceived as unjust and increases the probability of aggressive behavior. The physiological concomitants of anger are more sustained if their overt expression is prevented (Brosschot & Thayer, 1998). Depression can be produced by sustained deprivation, including a loss of social support accompanied by negative cognitions about self, and is typically accompanied by diminished activity (Lazarus, 1991). Depression has sometimes been thought of as anger turned inward, and depressed patients have been shown to have evidence of sympathetic arousal that is also characteristic of anger (Blazer, Kessler, McGonagle, & Swartz, 1994).

The presence of sustained anger or depression is predictive of increased mortality. For example, a recent longitudinal investigation of more than 800 clergy in the Religious Orders Study (mean age 75) found that suppressed anger and depression were both associated with increased death rates over a 4-year period, inde-

pendent of age, sex, age, education, smoking, alcohol use, and obesity (Wilson, Bienias, Mendes de Leon, Evans, & Bennett, 2003). By contrast, measures of externally directed negative affect, such as the tendency to be angry with others and to express anger overtly, were not predictors of mortality. This study confirmed and extended previous findings regarding negative affects and mortality in middle-aged men (e.g. Barefoot & Schroll, 1996; Eaker, Pinsky, & Castelli, 1992). The role of depression in disease has also been a focus in behavioral medicine (Health and Behavior, 2001), with considerable attention to its role in cardiovascular mortality (Smith & Gallo, 1999). Among a cohort of 2,847 participants, for example, evidence of depression increased the risk for cardiac mortality, independent of preexisting history of coronary heart disease (Penninx et al., 2001). For those participants with major depression, risk for cardiac mortality more than doubled (Penninx et al., 2001).

Negative Emotional States and Physiological Adaptations

Considerable research in behavioral medicine has explored effects of naturally occurring or experimentally induced negative emotional states on physiological functions. For example, high hostility has been associated with elevated ambulatory blood pressure during activities of daily living (Suarez & Blumenthal, 1991; Räikkönen & Matthews, Flory, & Owens, 1999). Chronic depression has long been associated with sustained activation of the hypothalamic-pituitary-adrenocortical (HPA) axis, resulting in increased concentrations of circulating cortisol (Brown, Varghese, & McEwan, 2004; O'Brien, Lloyd, McKeith, Gholkar, & Ferrier, 2004). Overstimulation of the HPA axis and excessive levels of circulating glucocorticoids have been associated with suppression of immune function, which can enhance susceptibility to infection (Sternberg, 2001).

Recent findings on brain electrical activity have renewed hope that negative emotional states can be characterized physiologically. Specifically, reliable individual differences in electrophysiological measures of prefrontal brain activity have been associated with negative affect (Tomarken, Davidson, Wheeler, & Kinney, 1992). In one study, persons with right-sided activation showed lower basal levels of natural killer (NK) cell activity and greater decreases in NK function during a period of naturally occurring stress (i.e., final examinations). By contrast, viewing a positive film clip that elicits positive affect was associated with a smaller change in NK cell activity (Davidson, Coe, Dolski, & Donzella, 1999). In addition, persons who were more depressed were more likely to show right prefrontal asymmetry (Henriques & Davidson, 1991) and to have weaker antibody response to influenza vaccination (Rosenkranz et al., 2003). The specific pathways responsible for the association of negative affect and suppression of immune function remain to be clarified but widespread connections to the immune system via the HPA axis have been identified. Animals with greater relative right-sided prefrontal activation showed higher basal levels of cortisol than animals exhibiting left prefrontal activation (Kalin, Larson, Shelton, & Davidson, 1998). These findings on brain and immune function support and extend other literature that describes associations of negative emotional states with periodontal infections (Merchant, Pitiphat, Ahmed, Kawachi, & Joshipura, 2003) and common colds (Takkouche, Regueira, & Gestal-Otero, 2001).

Negative Emotional States, Health Behaviors, and the Social Environment

The behavioral medicine literature provides compelling evidence that negative emotions are associated with increased risk for disease by means of adverse health habits, including cigarette smoking, physical inactivity, and alcohol consumption (Kubzansky & Kawachi, 2000; Kubzansky, Kawachi, Weiss, & Sparrow, 1998; Miller, Smith, Turner, Guijarro, & Hallet, 1996). In the University of North Carolina (UNC) Alumni study, for example, hostility assessed during the late teen years predicted increased likelihood of smoking, excessive alcohol intake, and higher levels of depression, up to 30 years later (Siegler et al., 2003). Depression and anger have also been associated with cigarette smoking, sedentary behavior (Brummett, Babyak et al., 2003; Kritz-Silverstein, Barrett-Connor, & Corbeau, 2001), and poorer adherence to care (Carney et al., 1995; DiMatteo, Lepper, & Croghan, 2000).

Lower levels of social support, or social isolation, are common among persons who report negative emotions, such as anger and depression (Williams, Barefoot, & Schneiderman, 2003) and constitute another possible determinant of disease. Several prospective cohort studies in the United States, Japan, and Scandinavia have demonstrated that people who are isolated from others are at increased risk of premature death (Health and Behavior, 2001). In the UNC Alumni study, hostility assessed during college years predicted perceptions of inadequate social support up to 30 years later, and changes in hostility from college to midlife were found to predict relative social isolation in midlife (Siegler et al., 2003). In another study using this same cohort, depressed mood was found to be associated with lower levels of social support (Brummett, Barefoot, Vitaliano, & Siegler, 2003). This association was greater among those with lower income. Low income or lower socioeconomic

status (SES) tended to cluster with low social support, resulting in multiple deficits in resources and increased vulnerability (Vitaliano, Dougherty, & Siegler, 1994). These multiple deficits can be viewed from the perspective of conservation of resources theory (Hobfoll, 1989), which argues that perceived stress, as well as depression and anger, can be evoked by loss of (or threat of loss of) resources (Hobfoll, Johnson, Ennis, & Jackson, 2003). The association of low SES with higher mortality is well documented (Health and Behavior, 2001), and low SES is significantly associated with negative emotional states, particularly depression (Lorant et al., 2003).

The Other Hemisphere: Positive Emotional States

Despite the preponderance of research on negative emotions and adverse health outcomes, a corollary literature exists that indicates that positive emotional states are associated with positive health outcomes, longevity, and well-being. Notably, findings from a longitudinal study of 678 Catholic nuns, ages 75–107, indicated that positive affect, reported early in adulthood, was associated with longevity (Danner, Snowdon, & Friesen, 2001). In this study, autobiographies of 180 nuns, composed at the age of 22, were scored for various types of emotional content. The analysis revealed that positive emotions predicted survival 6 decades later, prompting the investigators to conclude that "finding such a strong association of written positive emotional expression with longevity indicates a need for research that sheds light on the underlying mechanisms and mediators responsible for and associated with this relationship" (Danner et al., 2001, p. 812).

Further evidence of this association was found in a 2-year prospective cohort study in the southwestern United States (Ostir, Markides, Black, & Goodwin, 2000). The sample consisted of more than 2,000 Mexican-Americans, ages 65–99, who reported no functional limitations during a baseline interview. The participants provided information regarding positive and negative affect, health, assistance with daily living, mobility, and survival. Controlling for key variables, such as functional status, SES, major chronic conditions, negative health behaviors, and affect, those who reported more positive affect at baseline had higher rates of survival 2 years later. These findings are consistent with other recent longitudinal studies that showed that positive affect was associated with lower risk of AIDS mortality (Moskowitz, 2003) and more optimism with increased rates of survival (Maruta, Colligan, Malinchoc, & Offord, 2000; Peterson, Seligman, Yurko, Martin, & Friedman, 1998).

Positive Emotional States and Spirituality

Research on spirituality provides another resource for identification of positive emotions that may impact health. As reviewed by Emmons and Paloutzian (2003), spirituality involves a search for the sacred or "transcendent" in life (i.e., that which exists beyond material reality). Progress in this field to date has been limited by the need to generate acceptable operational definitions, measurement procedures, and research designs (Powell, Shahabi, & Thoresen, 2003).

A number of constructs have been identified in spirituality research that might be relevant to the study of positive emotions. *Gratitude* has been defined as "an estimate of gain coupled with the judgment that someone else is responsible for that gain" (Solomon, 1977, p. 316). *Forgiveness* has been considered in contrast to retaliatory instincts and associated physiological effects (McCullough, Emmons, & Tsang, 2002). *Humility* has been analyzed in contrast to *pride* with its accompanying defensiveness and antagonism (Bushman & Baumeister, 1998).

Research on the role of positive emotions associated with spirituality is only in its early stages, with some of the evidence from population-based studies supporting the hypothesis that church attendance is associated with decreased mortality, in part due to an association between church attendance and healthier lifestyles (reviewed by Powell et al., 2003). Consistent with the studies linking positive emotional states with survival cited in the previous section, one recent study, using a spirituality questionnaire, found that long-term survivors of HIV and AIDS had high scores on subscales entitled sense of peace, compassion for others, faith in God, and religious behavior (Ironson et al., 2002).

Positive Emotional States and Physiological Adaptations

Many of the same biological mechanisms by which negative affect might be associated with increased risk of morbidity and mortality are being investigated from the perspective of associations that may be protective and associated with survival. For example, recent findings on prefrontal brain activation asymmetry show that greater relative left-sided prefrontal activity, which is associated with positive affect, is also associated with larger increases in NK function in response to films that elicit positive affects, compared with those with greater relative right-sided activation (Davidson et al., 1999).

Significant relations between positive affect and immune function can be found in longitudinal studies in the natural environment. In a cohort study of more than 1,000 faculty and staff at a Spanish university, high scores on a test of positive affect (Watson, Clark, & Tellegen, 1988) were associated with less common cold infection (Takkouche et al., 2001). In a related study, 334 volunteers were rated on their tendency to experience positive as opposed to negative emotions. An increased positive emotional style was associated, in a dose-response manner, with a lower risk of developing a cold following a viral challenge (Cohen, Doyle, Turner, Alper, & Skoner, 2003). In a study of coping with the loss of a close relative to breast cancer, women who reported positive changes in goals emphasizing personal growth and striving for meaning in life and relationships during bereavement showed significant improvement in NK cell cytotoxicity (Bower, Kemeny, Taylor, & Fahey, 2003).

Positive emotions can speed recovery from physiological responses to stress (Fredrickson & Levenson, 1998). Participants in experiments who viewed films designed to elicit positive states, following exposure to an initial fear-arousing film, exhibited faster cardiovascular recovery than those who viewed neutral or sad films after the initial film. Different positive emotions were associated with differing cardiovascular recovery times such that participants who viewed a film considered to induce contentment showed faster cardiovascular recovery times than participants who viewed a comedy.

Further support for this association can be drawn from the literature on self-enhancers. As defined by Taylor and Brown (1988), self-enhancers are individuals who characterize themselves in a manner that emphasizes their positive qualities. Laboratory research shows that persons scoring high on self-enhancement have lower baseline cortisol levels, lower cardiovascular responses to stress, and more rapid cardiovascular recovery than those who are less self-enhancing (Taylor, Lerner, Sherman, Sage, & McDowell, 2003).

Positive Emotional States, Health Behaviors and the Social Environment

Positive emotions have been associated with increased likelihood of positive health behaviors, just as negative emotions are associated with maladaptive health behaviors. In a study in which volunteers were rated on their tendency to experience positive emotions, a positive emotional style was associated with a number of positive health habits, including better sleep, greater dietary nutrient intake, and more physical exercise (Cohen et al., 2003). Men who reported being more optimistic about their ability to slow the progression of their HIV disease practiced better health habits than did their more pessimistic counterparts (Taylor et al., 2000).

Although positive emotions are not routinely assessed in epidemiology, one study found that low scores on a depression scale predicted the practice of health behaviors such as exercise (Castro, Wilcox, O'Sullivan, Baumann, & King, 2002). In other studies, ratings of high life satisfaction, a variable related to positive emotions, was shown to be related to health-promoting behavior (King, Porter, & Rowe, 1994; King, Taylor, Haskell, & DeBusk, 1990). Self-efficacy expectations are also associated with psychological well-being (Bandura, 1997) and are significantly associated with increased adherence to physical activity recommendations in the elderly (Brassington, Atienza, Perczek, DiLorenzo, & King, 2002).

Another pathway linking positive affect and health is the role of positive emotions in social relationships. The influence of social support on health is well established, with significant positive relationships associated with lower mortality, greater resistance to illness, lower prevalence and incidence of coronary heart disease, and faster recovery from heart disease and heart surgery (see Salovey et al., 2000). People who report more positive emotions experience more social support (Fredrickson, 2000; Fredrickson & Levenson, 1998). Additional studies have shown significant associations between positive affect and estimates of the number of family members and friends who could be relied on for social support, as well as with the actual number of people who provided help over a 12-month period (Eckenrode et al. as cited in Cohen, 1988). Optimism, positive coping styles, a sense of mastery or control, and social support are associated with higher SES and have been proposed as potential mediators of the relation between SES and health (Taylor & Seeman, 1999).

Relations Between Positive and Negative Emotional States

Research into the adaptive functions of positive emotional states has found that positive and negative emotions are not necessarily opposite ends of a single continuum of mood. Evidence that negative and positive emotions are not always mutually exclusive has been found in both psychological (e.g., Billings, Folkman, Acree, & Moskowitz, 2000; Diener & Emmons, 1985; Russell & Barrett, 1999) and physiological research (Cacioppo, Berntson, & Gardner, 1999).

It is generally acknowledged that negative affect is likely to occur during periods of chronic stress. Of more recent origin, however, is the idea that positive affect can also occur during chronic stress and that negative and positive emotions can be experienced at the same time (Folkman, 1997; Folkman & Moskowitz, 2000; Wortman & Silver, 1987). It is possible that the presence of positive affect during chronic stress may ameliorate the deleterious effects of negative affect.

For example, the ability to sustain a positive mood during the stress of caregiving for a seriously ill partner was associated with more rapid recovery following subsequent bereavement (Folkman, Chesney, Collette, Boccellari, & Cooke, 1996). Intriguing evidence also exists that positive and negative affects may operate on separate neurophysiological systems and may produce independent patterns of autonomic activation (Cacioppo, Berntson, Larsen, Poehlmann, & Ito, 2000). These studies illustrate the need for more detailed study of the ways in which positive and negative emotions can interact.

Interventions to Enhance Positive Emotional States

An extensive body of research has evaluated interventions designed to reduce the harmful health effects of stress and negative affect (Smith & Ruiz, 2002). One of these interventions, coping effectiveness training (CET; Chesney, Chambers, Taylor, Johnson, & Folkman, 2003; Chesney & Folkman, 1994; Chesney, Folkman, & Chambers, 1996; Folkman & Chesney, 1995), utilizes stress and coping theory (Folkman et al., 1991; Lazarus & Folkman, 1984) and elements of cognitive-behavioral stress management interventions (Antoni et al., 1991; Fawzy, Namir, & Wolcott, 1989). Delivered in a group treatment context, CET focuses on training individuals to choose among coping strategies to promote adaptive coping and reduce distress.

When it was first designed, CET drew attention to positive emotions by encouraging participants to acknowledge and share positive experiences in the treatment groups, keep track of positive events at the end of the day, use humor in coping, and identify sources of meaning in their lives. A randomized clinical trial of CET among 149 men living with HIV and AIDS (mean age 39, 82% White) showed that, when compared to control participants, participants receiving CET demonstrated significantly greater decreases in the Perceived Stress Scale (Cohen, Karmarck, & Mermelstein, 1983), State Anxiety (Spielberger, Gorsuch, & Lushene, 1974), and greater increases in a measure of coping self-efficacy during the 3-month intervention phase, $F(1, 124)$[1] statistics ranged from 4.15 to 6.06, all ps < .05. Multiple regression analyses indicated that the decreases in perceived stress and burnout were mediated by increases in coping self-efficacy. Of particular relevance here, when compared to control participants, CET participants also showed a statistical trend for greater increases in positive affect (Bradburn & Caplovitz, 1965) during the intervention phase, $F(1,$

---

[1]All F statistics for group comparisons were calculated using analysis of covariance (ANCOVA), controlling for preintervention scores.

124) = 2.81, p = .09, that were maintained at the 6- and 12-month assessment points, $F(1, 88) = 4.44$, $p = .04$ (Chesney et al., 2003).

Based on the findings of the first trial of CET, the intervention was revised to include more specific training to enhance positive affect and meaning in life. Exercises were added to the group-based intervention to train participants to recognize small positive experiences that occur in everyday life; acknowledge the positive aspects of those experiences, however small; describe the experiences to others; and identify how the event or experience is meaningful in terms of personal values, goals, or purpose. The revised form of CET was tested in a randomized clinical trial with 199 men living with HIV and AIDS (mean age 42, 77% White) who met inclusion criteria indicating elevated negative affect.

The design of the second trial was similar to that of the previous study (Chesney et al., 2003) but focused more on measures of positive affect with the inclusion of a short form of the Positive States of Mind Scale (Horowitz, Adler, & Kegeles, 1988) and the Stress-Related Personal Growth Scale (Park & Blumberg, 2002). The latter scale assesses the impact of stress on personal meaning with items such as "I learned to find more meaning in life" and "I learned that I have something of value to teach others about my life." During the 3-month intervention phase, when compared to control participants, the CET participants showed significantly greater decreases in perceived stress, burnout, and negative affect (Bradburn & Caplovitz, 1965) and significantly greater increases in coping self-efficacy, $F(1, 196)$ statistics ranged from 3.66 to 7.40, all $ps < .05$. Of particular importance in this second study, significant treatment group differences were found for positive states of mind, $F(1, 196) = 4.47$, $p = .04$, and personal growth, $F(1, 196) = 7.50$, $p = .007$, immediately after the 3-month intervention. As shown in Figures 1a and 1b, these group differences were maintained throughout the 9-month follow-up phase, $F(1, 169) = 6.26$, $p = .01$ for positive states of mind and $F(1, 169) = 8.77$, $p = .004$ for personal growth. These findings indicate that cognitive interventions can enhance positive affect and that these improvements can be sustained over time.

Further evidence of the effects of behavioral intervention on positive emotional states is provided by research suggesting that "mindfulness meditation" (Kabat-Zinn et al., 1992) may be associated with changes in left-sided anterior brain activity that are associated with positive emotional states (Davidson et al., 2003). Not only were greater effects observed in the meditators compared to waiting list controls, but the meditators also showed increases in antibody titers to influenza vaccine. This investigation, considered in conjunction with the reports of CET, demonstrates that positive states can be increased with behavioral inter-

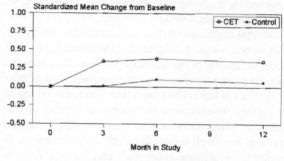

a. Positive States of Mind Scale

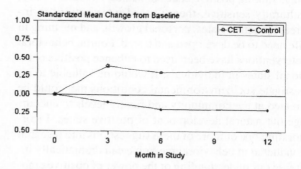

b. Personal Growth Scale

Figure 1. **Standardized mean change from baseline for the positive affect scales: Comparison of the CET and control groups during the maintenance phase.** *Note:* **Means for month 3, 6, and 12 are adjusted for the baseline score.**

vention and that the changes that are produced may be associated with salutary health effects.

Investigators studying the effects of a cognitive-behavioral stress management intervention similar to CET on early-stage breast cancer patients came to a similar conclusion (Cruess et al., 2000). Following the intervention, women showed greater reductions in cortisol than did waiting-list controls. These reductions, although not associated with changes in distress scores, were significantly associated with increases in perceived positive gains or personal growth from the experience of breast cancer. The investigators concluded that the effect of the intervention on cortisol was mediated by increases in patients' reporting positive benefit or growth from their cancer experience.

Conclusion

We have provided empirical evidence that we hope will encourage researchers in behavioral medicine to explore the other hemisphere in emotional life—that of positive affect. Pathways exist by which positive emotions may influence health and well-being, either directly through physiological changes or indirectly through health behaviors and social support. Positive and negative affects can be observed in the same person at the same time. Increasing understanding of positive affect and its influence on health cannot be achieved by studying only the absence of negative affect, anger, or depression.

Several implications of this recommendation for the field of behavioral medicine should be noted. First, although a handful of measures of positive affect is available, far more is known about the measurement of negative affect in behavioral medicine. Thus, a need exists for further development of reliable and valid instruments for the assessment of positive states, affect, emotion and well-being. Second, more research is needed to investigate conceptual and biological pathways linking positive states to health outcomes. Third, culturally sensitive, theory-based interventions to increase positive states, personal growth, and meaning in life need to be developed and tested. Fourth, behavioral interventions have been used to enhance positive emotional states in individuals. It would be valuable to investigate socioenvironmental conditions that could be created at the community and family levels to encourage the natural development of positive states. Incorporating one or more of these suggestions into research conducted in behavioral medicine can dramatically increase our understanding of the power of positive emotions to significantly impact health and well-being.

In behavioral medicine, we have a choice. We can focus on the weeds in the garden, understand how they take root, and study their impact on the environment or we can plant a few flowers, understand how they take root, and help them grow.

References

Alexander, F. (1939). Emotional factors in essential hypertension. *Psychosomatic Medicine, 1,* 173–179.

Antoni, M. H., Baggett, L., Ironson, G., LaPerriere, A., August, S., Klimas, N., Schneiderman, N., & Fletcher, M. H. (1991). Cognitive-behavioral stress management intervention buffers distress responses and immunologic changes following notification of HIV–1 seropositivity. *Journal of Consulting and Clinical Psychology, 59,* 906–915.

Bandura, A. (1997). *Self-efficacy: The exercise of control.* New York: Freeman.

Barefoot, J. C., & Schroll, M. (1996). Symptoms of depression, acute myocardial infarction, and total mortality in a community sample. *Circulation, 93,* 1976–1980.

Billings, D. W., Folkman, S., Acree, M., & Moskowitz, J. T. (2000). Coping and physical health during caregiving: The roles of positive and negative affect. *Journal of Personality and Social Psychology, 79,* 131–142.

Blazer, D. G., Kessler, R. C., McGonagle, K. A., & Swartz, M. S. (1994). The prevalence and distribution of major depression in a national community sample: The National Comorbidity Survey. *American Journal of Psychiatry, 151,* 979–986.

Bower, J. E., Kemeny, M. E., Taylor, S. E., & Fahey, J. L. (2003). Finding positive meaning and its association with natural killer cell cytotoxicity among participants in a bereavement-related disclosure intervention. *Annals of Behavioral Medicine, 25,* 146–155.

Bradburn, N., & Caplovitz, D. (1965). *Reports on happiness: A pilot study of behavior related to mental health.* Chicago: Aldine.

Brassington, G. S., Atienza, A. A., Perczek, R. E., DiLorenzo, T. M., & King, A. C. (2002). Intervention-related cognitive versus social mediators of exercise adherence in the elderly. *American Journal of Preventative Medicine, 23*(2 Suppl), 80–86.

Brosschot, J. F., & Thayer, J. F. (1998). Anger inhibition, cardiovascular recovery, and vagal function: A model of the link between hostility and cardiovascular disease. *Annals of Behavioral Medicine, 20,* 326–332.

Brown, E. S., Varghese, F. P., & McEwen, B. S. (2004). Association of depression with medical illness: Does cortisol play a role? *Biological Psychiatry, 55,* 1–9.

Brummett, B. H., Babyak, M. A., Siegler, I. C., Mark, D. B., Williams, R. B., & Barefoot, J. C. (2003). Effect of smoking and sedentary behavior on the association between depressive symptoms and mortality from coronary heart disease. *American Journal of Cardiology, 92,* 529–532.

Brummett, B. H., Barefoot, J. C., Vitaliano, P. P., & Siegler, I. C. (2003). Associations among social support, income, and symptoms of depression in an educated sample: The UNC Alumni Heart Study. *International Journal of Behavioral Medicine, 10,* 239–250.

Bush, D. E., Ziegelstein, R. C., Tayback, M., Richter, D., Stevens, S., Zahalsky, H., & Fauerbach, J. A. (2001). Even minimal symptoms of depression increase mortality risk after acute myocardial infarction. *American Journal of Cardiology, 88,* 337–341.

Bushman, B. J., & Baumeister, R. (1998). Threatened egotism, narcissism, self-esteem and direct and displaced aggression: Does self-love or self-hate lead to violence? *Journal of Personality and Social Psychology, 75,* 219–229.

Cacioppo, J. T., Berntson, G. G., & Gardner, W. L. (1999). The affect system has parallel and integrative processing components: Form follows function. *Journal of Personality and Social Psychology, 76,* 805–819.

Cacioppo, J. T., Berntson, G. G., Larsen, J. T., Poehlmann, K. M., & Ito, T. A. (2000). The psychophysiology of emotion. In M. Lewis & J. M. Haviland-Jones (Eds.), *Handbook of emotions* (pp. 173–191). New York: Guilford.

Cannon, W. B. (1929). *Bodily changes in pain, hunger, fear and rage.* New York: Appleton.

Carney, R. M., Rich, M. W., Tevelde, A., Saini, J., Clark, K., & Jaffe, A. S. (1995). Depression as a risk factor or cardiac events in established coronary heart disease: A review of possible mechanisms. *Annals of Behavioral Medicine, 17,* 142–149.

Castro, C. M., Wilcox, S., O'Sullivan, P., Baumann, K., & King, A. C. (2002). An exercise program for women who are caring for relatives with dementia. *Psychosomatic Medicine, 64,* 458–468.

Chesney, M. A., Chambers, D. B., Taylor, J. M., Johnson, L. S., & Folkman, S. (2003). Coping effectiveness training for men living with HIV: Results from a randomized clinical trial testing a group-based intervention. *Psychosomatic Medicine, 65,* 1038–1046.

Chesney, M. A., & Folkman, S. (1994). Psychological impact of HIV disease and implications for intervention. *Psychiatric Clinics of North America, 17,* 163–182.

Chesney, M., Folkman, S., & Chambers, D. (1996). Coping effectiveness training for men living with HIV: Preliminary findings. *International Journal of STD & AIDS, 7*(Suppl 2), 75–82.

Cohen, S. (1988). Psychosocial models of the role of social support in the etiology of physical disease. *Health Psychology, 7,* 269–297.

Cohen, S., Doyle, W. J., Turner, R., Alper, C. M., & Skoner, D. P. (2003). Sociability and susceptibility to the common cold. *Psychological Science, 14,* 389–395.

Cohen, S., Karmarck, T., & Mermelstein, R. (1983). A global measure of perceived stress. *Journal of Health and Social Behavior, 24,* 385–396.

Cruess, D. G., Antoni, M. H., McGregor, B. A., Kilbourn, K. M, Boyers, A. E., Alferi, S. M., Carver, C. S., & Kumar, M. (2000). Cognitive-behavioral stress management reduces serum cortisol by enhancing benefit finding among women being treated for early stage breast cancer. *Psychosomatic Medicine, 62,* 304–308

Danner, D. D., Snowdon, D. A., & Friesen, W. V. (2001). Positive emotions in early life and longevity: Findings from the nun study. *Journal of Personality and Social Psychology, 80,* 804–813.

Davidson, R. J., Coe, C. C., Dolski, I., & Donzella, B. (1999). Individual differences in prefrontal activation asymmetry predict natural killer cell activity at rest and in response to challenge. *Brain, Behavior, and Immunity, 13,* 93–108.

Davidson, R. J., Kabat-Zinn, J., Schumacher, J., Rosenkranz, M., Muller, D., Santorelli, S. F., Urbanowski, F., Harrington, A., Bonus, K., & Sheridan, J. F. (2003). Alterations in brain and immune function produced by mindfulness meditation. *Psychosomatic Medicine, 65,* 564–570.

Diener, E., & Emmons, R. A. (1985). The independence of positive and negative affect. *Journal of Personality and Social Psychology, 47,* 1105–1117.

DiMatteo, M. R., Lepper, H. S., & Croghan, T. W. (2000). Depression is a risk factor for noncompliance with medical treatment: Meta-analysis of the effects of anxiety and depression on patient adherence. *Archives of Internal Medicine, 160,* 2101–2107.

Eaker, E. D., Pinsky, J., & Castelli, W. P. (1992). Myocardial infarction and coronary death among women: Psychosocial predictors from a 20-year follow-up of women in the Framingham Study. *American Journal of Epidemiology, 135,* 854–864.

Emmons, R. A., & Paloutzian, R. F. (2003). The psychology of religion. *Annual Review of Psychology, 54,* 377–402.

Engel, G. L. (1971). Sudden and rapid death during psychological stress. *Annals of Internal Medicine, 74,* 771–782.

Fawzy, F. I., Namir, S., & Wolcott, D. L. (1989). Structured group intervention model for AIDS patients. *Psychiatric Medicine, 7*(2), 35–45.

Folkman, S. (1997). Positive psychological states and coping with severe stress. *Social Science & Medicine, 45,* 1207–1221.

Folkman, S., & Chesney, M. (1995). Coping with HIV infection. In M. Stein & A. Baum (Eds.), *Chronic diseases* (pp. 115–134). Mahwah, NJ: Lawrence Erlbaum Associates, Inc.

Folkman, S., Chesney, M. A., Collette, L., Boccellari, A., & Cooke, M. (1996). Postbereavement depressive mood and its prebereavement predictors in HIV + and HIV- gay men. *Journal of Personality and Social Psychology, 70,* 336–348.

Folkman, S., Chesney, M., McKusick, L., Ironson, G., Johnson, D., & Coates, T. (1991). Translating coping theory into intervention. In J. Eckenrode (Ed.), *The social context of stress* (pp. 239–260). New York: Plenum.

Folkman, S., & Moskowitz, J. T. (2000). Positive affect and the other side of coping. *American Psychologist, 55,* 647–654.

Frank, J. D. (1961). *Persuasion and healing.* New York: Schocken.

Fredrickson, B. L. (2000). *Cultivating positive emotions to optimize health and well-being.* Retrieved March 27, 2003 from the World Wide Web: http://www.journals.apa.org/prevention/volume3/pre0030001a.html

Fredrickson, B. L., & Levenson, R. W. (1998). Positive emotions speed recovery from the cardiovascular sequelae of negative emotions. *Cognition and Emotion, 12,* 191–220.

Gorham, G. (1994). Mind-body dualism and the Harvey-Descartes controversy. *Journal of History of Ideas, 55,* 211–234.

Henriques, J., & Davidson, R. J. (1991). Left frontal hypoactivation in depression. *Journal of Abnormal Psychology, 99,* 22–31.

Hobfoll, S. E. (1989). Conservation of resources: A new attempt at conceptualizing stress. *American Psychologist, 44,* 513–524.

Hobfoll, S. E., Johnson, R. J., Ennis, N., & Jackson, A. P. (2003). Resource loss, resource gain, and emotional outcomes among inner city women. *Journal of Personality and Social Psychology, 84,* 632–43.

Horowitz, M., Adler, N., & Kegeles, S. (1988). A scale for measuring the occurrence of positive states of mind: A preliminary report. *Psychosomatic Medicine, 50,* 477–483.

IOM (Institute of Medicine) (2001). *Health and behavior: The interplay of biological, behavioral, and societal influences.* Washington, DC: National Academy Press.

Ironson, G, Solomon, G. F., Balbin, E. G., O'Cleirigh, C, George, A., Kumar, M., Larson, D., & Woods, T. E. (2002). The Ironson-Woods Spirituality/Religiousness Index is associated with long survival, health behaviors, less distress, and low cortisol in people with HIV/AIDS. *Annals of Behavioral Medicine, 24,* 34–48.

Kabat-Zinn, J., Massion, A. O., Kristeller, J., Peterson, L. G., Fletcher, K. E., Pbert, L., Lenderking, W. R., & Santorelli, S. F. (1992). Effectiveness of a meditation-based stress reduction program in the treatment of anxiety disorders. *American Journal Of Psychiatry, 149,* 936–943.

Kalin, N., Larson, C., Shelton, S., & Davidson, R. (1998). Asymmetric frontal brain activity, cortisol, and behavior associated with fearful temperament in Rhesus monkeys. *Behavioral Neuroscience, 112,* 286–292.

King, A. C., Porter, L. A., & Rowe, M. A. (1994). Functional, social, and emotional outcomes in women and men in the first year following coronary artery bypass surgery. *Journal of Women's Health, 3,* 347–354.

King, A. C., Taylor, C. B., Haskell, W. L., & DeBusk, R. F. (1990). Identifying strategies for increasing employee physical activity levels: Findings from the Stanford/Lockheed Exercise Survey. *Health Education Quarterly, 17,* 269–285.

Kritz-Silverstein, D., Barrett-Connor, E., & Corbeau, C. (2001). Cross-sectional and prospective study of exercise and depressed mood in the elderly: The Rancho Bernardo study. *American Journal of Epidemiology, 153,* 596–603.

Kubzansky, L. D., & Kawachi, I. (2000). Going to the heart of the matter: Do negative emotions cause coronary heart disease? *Journal of Psychosomatic Research, 48*(4–5), 323–337.

Kubzansky, L. D., Kawachi, I., Weiss, S. T., & Sparrow, D. (1998). Anxiety and coronary heart disease: A synthesis of epidemiological, psychological, and experimental evidence. *Annals of Behavioral Medicine, 20,* 47–58.

Lazarus, R. S. (1991). *Emotion and adaptation.* New York: Oxford University Press.

Lazarus, R., & Folkman, S. (1984). *Stress, appraisal, and coping.* New York: Springer.

Lorant, V., Deliege, D., Eaton, W., Robert, A., Philippot, P., & Ansseau, M. (2003). Socioeconomic inequalities in depression: A meta-analysis. *American Journal of Epidemiology, 157,* 98–112.

Maruta, T., Colligan, R. C., Malinchoc, M., & Offord, K. P. (2000). Optimists vs pessimists: Survival rate among medical patients over a 30-year period. *Mayo Clinic Proceedings, 75,* 140–143.

McCullough, M. E., Emmons, R. A., & Tsang, J. (2002). The grateful disposition: A conceptual and empirical topography. *Journal of Personality and Social Psychology, 82,* 112–127.

Merchant, A., Pitiphat, W., Ahmed, B., Kawachi, I., & Joshipura, K. (2003). A prospective study of social support, anger expression and risk of periodontitis in men. *Journal of the American Dental Association, 134,* 1591–1596.

Miller, T. Q., Smith, T. W., Turner, C. W., Guijarro, M. L., & Hallet, A. J. (1996). A meta-analytic review of research on hostility and physical health. *Psychological Bulletin, 119,* 322–348.

Moskowitz, J. T. (2003). Positive affect predicts lower risk of AIDS mortality. *Psychosomatic Medicine, 65,* 620–626.

O'Brien, J. T., Lloyd, A., McKeith, I., Gholkar, A., & Ferrier N. (2004). A longitudinal study of hippocampal volume, cortisol levels, and cognition in older depressed subjects. *American Journal of Psychiatry, 161,* 2081–290.

Ostir, G. V., Markides, K. S., Black, S. A., & Goodwin, J. S. (2000). Emotional well-being predicts subsequent functional independence and survival. *Journal American Geriatric Society, 48*, 473–478.

Park, C. L., & Blumberg, C. J. (2002). Disclosing trauma through writing: Testing the meaning-making hypothesis. *Cognitive Therapy and Research, 26*, 597–616.

Penninx, B. W., Beekman, A. T., Honig, A., Deeg, D. J., Schoevers, R. A., van Eijk, J. T., & van Tilburg, W. (2001). Depression and cardiac mortality: Results from a community-based longitudinal study. *Archives of General Psychiatry, 58*, 221–227.

Peterson, C., Seligman, M. E. P., Yurko, K. H., Martin, L. R., & Friedman, H. S. (1998). Catastrophizing and untimely death. *Psychological Science, 9*, 127–130.

Powell, L. H., Shahabi, L., & Thoresen, C. E. (2003). Religion and spirituality: Linkages to physical health. *American Psychologist, 58*, 36–52

Räikkönen, K., Matthews, K. A., Flory, J. D., & Owens, J. F. (1999). Effects of hostility on ambulatory blood pressure and mood during daily living in healthy adults. *Health Psychology, 18*, 44–53.

Rosenkranz, M. A., Jackson, D. C., Dalton, K. M., Dolski, I., Ryff, C. D., Singer, B. H., Muller, D., Kalin, N. H., & Davidson, R. J. (2003). Affective style and in vivo immune response: Neurobehavioral mechanisms. *Proceedings of the National Academy of Science of the United States of America, 100*, 11148–11152.

Rosenman, R. H., Brand, R. J., Jenkins, D., Friedman, M., Straus, R., & Wurm, M. (1975). Coronary heart disease in Western Collaborative Group Study. Final follow-up experience of 8–1/2 years. *Journal of the American Medical Association, 233*, 872–877.

Russell, J. A., & Barrett, L. F. (1999). Core affect, prototypical emotional episodes, and other things called emotion: Dissecting the elephant. *Journal of Personality and Social Psychology, 76*, 805–819.

Salovey, P., Rothman, A. J., Detweiler, J. B., & Steward, W. T. (2000). Emotional states and physical health. *American Psychologist, 55*, 110–121.

Selye, H. (1956). *The stress of life.* New York: McGraw-Hill.

Siegler, I. C., Costa, P. T., Brummett, B. H., Helms, M. J., Barefoot, J. C., Williams, R. B., Dahlstrom, W. G., Kaplan, B. H., Vitaliano, P. P., Nichaman, M. Z., Day, R. S., & Rimer, B. K. (2003). Patterns of change in hostility from college to midlife in the UNC Alumni Heart Study predict high-risk status. *Psychosomatic Medicine, 65*, 738–745.

Silverman, M. E., Murray, T. J., & Brian, C. S. (2003). *The quotable Osler.* Philadelphia: American College of Physicians.

Smith, T. W., & Gallo, L. C. (1999). Hostility and cardiovascular reactivity during marital interaction. *Psychosomatic Medicine, 61*, 436–445.

Smith, T. W., & Ruiz, J. M. (2002). Psychosocial influences on the development and course of coronary heart disease: Current status and implications for research and practice. *Journal of Consulting and Clinical Psychology, 70*, 548–68

Solomon, R. C. (1977). *The passions.* New York: Anchor.

Spielberger, C. D., Gorsuch, R. L., & Lushene, R. E. (1974). *STAI manual for the state-trait anxiety inventory.* Palo Alto, CA: Consulting Psychologists Press.

Sternberg, E. M. (2001). Neuroendocrine regulation of autoimmune/inflammatory disease. *Journal of Endocrinology, 169*, 429–435.

Suarez, E. C., & Blumenthal, J. A. (1991). Ambulatory blood pressure responses during daily life in high and low hostile patients with a recent myocardial infarction. *Journal of Cardiopulmonary Rehabilitation, 11*, 169–175.

Takkouche, B., Regueira, C., & Gestal-Otero, J. J. (2001). A cohort study of stress and the common cold. *Epidemiology, 12*, 345–349.

Taylor, S. E., & Brown, J. D. (1988). Illusion and well-being: A social psychological perspective on mental health. *Psychological Bulletin, 103*, 193–210.

Taylor, S. E., Kemeny, M. E., Reed, G. M., Bower, J. E., & Gruenewald, T. L. (2000). Psychological resources, positive illusions, and health. *American Psychologist, 55*, 99–109.

Taylor, S. E., Lerner, J. S., Sherman, D. K., Sage, R. M., & McDowell, N. K. (2003). Are self-enhancing cognitions associated with healthy or unhealthy biological profiles? *Journal of Personality and Social Psychology, 85*, 605–615.

Taylor, S. E., & Seeman, T. E. (1999). Psychosocial resources and the SES-health relationship. *Annals of the New York Academy of Sciences, 896*, 210–225.

Tomarken, A. J., Davidson, R. J., Wheeler, R. E., & Kinney, L. (1992). Psychometric properties of resting anterior EEG asymmetry: Temporal stability and internal consistency. *Psychophysiology, 29*, 576–592.

Vitaliano, P., Dougherty, C., & Siegler, I. C. (1994). *Biopsychosocial risks for cardiovascular disease in spouse caregivers of persons with Alzheimer's disease.* New York: Springer.

Watson, D., Clark, L. A., & Tellegen, A. (1988). Development and validation of brief measures of positive and negative affect: The PANAS scales. *Journal of Personality and Social Psychology, 6*, 1063–1070.

Williams, R. B., Barefoot, J. C., & Schneiderman, N. (2003). Psychosocial risk factors for cardiovascular disease: More than one culprit at work. *Journal of the American Medical Association, 290*, 2190–2192.

Wilson, R. S., Bienias, J. L., Mendes de Leon, C. F., Evans, D. A., & Bennett, D. A. (2003). Negative affect and mortality in older persons. *American Journal of Epidemiology, 158*, 827–835.

Wortman, C., & Silver, R. (1987). Coping with irrevocable loss. In G. R. Vandenbos & B. K. Bryand (Eds.), *Cataclysms, crises and catastrophes: Psychology in action* (pp. 189–235). Washington, DC: American Psychological Association.

International Journal of Behavioral Medicine
2005, Vol. 12, No. 2, 59–65

The Psychobiology of Emotion: The Role of the Oxytocinergic System

Kerstin Uvnäs-Moberg, Ingemar Arn, and David Magnusson

A necessary condition for the individual's survival is the capacity for mental, behavioral, and physiological adaptation to external and internal conditions. Consequently, the integrated organism strives to maintain a dynamic, functional balance and integrity under varying conditions. Effective individual adaptation processes are basically dependent on the functioning of the integrated psychophysiological system.

In humans, the brain plays a fundamental role in these processes. It serves the adaptation of individuals to current and anticipated conditions by selecting, interpreting, and transforming information into mental, behavioral, and physiological responses. In doing so, the incoming information is linked to existing structures of emotions, values, and goals. Consequently, the interpretation of external information may vary and become subjective depending on an individual's present and past experiences (see e.g., Magnusson, 2003).

Hitherto, empirical research has been mainly concerned with the aspect of the psychophysiological system, which is activated in situations that are perceived by the individual as threatening, harmful, or demanding and in which the fight–flight and stress responses described by Cannon (1929) and Selye (1976) play an important role.

The aim of this article is to draw attention to a component of the psychophysiological system, the calm and connection system, underlying well-being and socialization. By including this new system, the model of the integrated individual becomes more complete and it enriches the understanding of emotional aspects of brain functioning.

Key words: calmness, connection response, oxytocin, emotions, positive development

Fight and Flight and Stress Responses

In classical studies, Cannon (1929) demonstrated how the sympathetic nervous system was activated and the catecholamines, epinephrine (EPI) and norepinephrine (NE), were released in response to stimuli and situations, which the individual experiences as demanding, harmful, or threatening. The more sustained stress-related effect of corticosteroids released from the adrenal cortex in response to adrenocorticotropic hormone (ACTH), secreted from the pituitary, was advocated by Selye (1976). Together these chemicals were supposed to prepare the body for fight or flight. The fight and flight response consists of both behav-

ioral and physiological adaptations such as arousal, anxiety, aggression, increased cardiovascular activity, and elevated blood glucose levels. Corticotrophin-releasing factor (CRF) and vasopressin from the hypothalamus and the brainstem NE system emanating in the locus ceruleus (LC) play important regulatory roles of both the behavioral and physiological components of the fight–flight response at the level of the central nervous system (CNS; Chrousos & Gold, 1992; Mason, 1968a, 1968b).

From the beginning, the fight–flight reactions were mainly supposed to be activated in situations that threaten the survival of the organism. Pain and tissue damage, cold and hunger, and environmental dangers are examples of somatic triggers that activate the defense and stress mechanisms in the hypothalamus and the brainstem and also the emotional state of fear in the amygdala.

Modern humans may, however, react with stress or defense reactions in response to a much wider range of stimuli via the cognitive–emotional act of interpretation. If a person meets a situation that he or she experiences or perceives as new, harmful, threatening, or demanding, the stress system may be activated

Kerstin Uvnäs-Moberg and Ingemar Arn, Department of Physiology and Pharmacology, Division of Pharmacology, Karolinska Institutet, Stockholm, Sweden and at the Department of Animal Environment and Health, Swedish University of Agricultural Sciences, Skara, Sweden; David Magnusson, Department of Psychology, Stockholm University, Stockholm, Sweden.

Correspondence concerning this article should be addressed to Kerstin Uvnäs-Moberg, Department of Physiology and Pharmacology, Division of Pharmacology, Karolinska Institutet Stockholm, Sweden. E-mail: Kerstin.Uvnas-Moberg@fyfa.ki.se via the amygdala-hippocampal complex. Emotional states of fear, anxiety, or both as well as the cascade of stress-related physiological events are likely to accompany this perceptual cognitive–emotional interplay (Chrousos & Gold, 1992).

Calm and Connection

The proposition presented here is that there is an analogous integrated psychophysiological pattern that is characterized by well-being, calm, and positive social interactions. The corresponding physiological pattern consists of relaxation of muscles, decreased cortisol levels, and cardiovascular activity, as well as enhanced activity in the gastrointestinal tract promoting digestion and anabolism. The vagal, parasympathetic nervous system is activated and the hypothalamic-pituitary-adrenocortical (HPA) axis and the sympatho-adreno-medullary (SAM) system are shut down. At the central level, hypothalamic oxytocin plays an important integrative role, as further elaborated on later (Uvnäs-Moberg, 1997, 1998a, 1998b).

We suggest that this pattern, which will be referred to as calm and connection (Uvnäs-Moberg, 2003), can be triggered not only by calming physiological stimuli such as nonnoxious somatosensory stimulation (e.g., in response to touch and warmth, see later) but also by environmental and psychological triggers of analogous type.

In contrast to the immediate reactions of the fight and flight and response, the physiological expressions and the subjective feelings of calm and connection appear with some delay. The subjective signs are subtle

and sometimes more easily defined by their absence than by their presence. However, it has a distinct psychophysiological pattern, and its expression has been experimentally demonstrated in a number of behavioral and physiological model systems. Pulse rate and blood pressure are kept at a low, healthy, and balanced level, and the vagally controlled gastrointestinal tract is activated, promoting digestion and storing of nutrients. Growth and restorative processes are stimulated. Energy would rather be used for anabolic purposes than for muscular or thermogenic activity. Behaviorally, reduced arousal and the development of calm prevail. Positive, social interaction is promoted. Subjectively, this state might be related to a sense of well-being and relaxation. This state should not, however, be confused with euphoria, which is a more intense feeling of joy and reward (Uvnäs-Moberg, 1997, 1998a, 1998b).

Reni's painting of the Madonna and Child captures some of the most significant features of the state of calm and connection (Figure 1). The painting illustrates that this state contains both an individual and an interactive component. The Madonna is relaxed, calm, content, happy, peaceful, warm, open, generous, empathic, and friendly. In the interaction with the child, she displays closeness, trust, loyalty, giving and receiving, and love. Individual boundaries are erased, and a sense of unity prevails. Needless to say, the Madonna with the child is just one example of this state, which can be experienced in a variety of different situations, independent of sex and age. Such situations range from the well-being and physiological relaxation induced by a hot bath, by being part of a social group, or by receiving massage.

Figure 1. The Madonna with her child, as an expression of the individual and the interactive aspects of eustasis. ("Madonna and Child" by Guido Reni, 1575–1642).

Oxytocin as an Agent in the Calm and Connection Response

We propose that oxytocin plays an important integrating factor in the mediation of calm and connection. Oxytocin was originally described as a female hormone, because it plays important roles in labor and lactation. The effect spectrum of oxytocin is, however, much broader than previously thought, and oxytocin is released in a wide range of situations in both females and males (for references see later).

Oxytocin is produced in the paraventricular nucleus (PVN) and supraoptic nucleus (SON) of the hypothalamus. Magnocellular oxytocinergic neurons in these nuclei project to the posterior pituitary from which oxytocin can be secreted to exert its well-known hormonal effects during labor and lactation. Parvocellular oxytocinergic neurons of the PVN, on the other hand, ramify within the brain to reach limbic, medullary, and spinal areas. Thus, for example, oxytocin fibers reach the amygdala, the nucleus tractus solitarius (NTS), the vagal motor nucleus (DMX), the LC, and the raphe nuclei of the brainstem. The oxytocin nerves have a similar projection pattern in females and males (Sofroniew, 1983). In females, both the release of oxytocin and the number of oxytocin receptors is increased by estrogens via receptors of the beta and alpha type, respectively (Choleris et al., 2003). A release of oxytocin in the amygdala has been demonstrated after suckling in sheep and rats and into the spinal fluid in response to vaginal stimulation suggesting that oxytocin is released from nerve terminals in the specific brain regions receiving oxytocinergic nerve projections (Kendrick, Keverne, Baldwin, & Sharman, 1986; Wigger & Neumann, 2002; Sansone et al., 2002).

Oxytocin thus acts both as a hormone and a neuropeptide, and only data of relevance for the hypothesis presented in this paper is summarized below (Richard, Moos, & Freund-Mercier, 1991). It has, for example, been shown that oxytocin stimulates various interactive behaviors such as maternal, sexual, and other social behaviors. It also promotes attachment or bonding between mother and infants and between females and males of monogamous species (Carter, 1998; Insel, 1992). Moreover, oxytocin may produce anxiolytic-like or sedative effects and increase pain threshold. It also influences cardiovascular and gastrointestinal function (Ågren, Lundeberg, Uvnäs-Moberg, & Sato, 1995; MacCarthy & Allemus, 1997; Uvnäs-Moberg, Ahlenius, Hillegaart, & Alster, 1994; Uvnäs-Moberg, Alster, Hillegaart, & Ahlenius, 1992; Uvnäs-Moberg, Bruzelius, Alster, & Lundeberg, 1993; Windle, Shanks, Lightman, & Ingram, 1997). Some of the effects of oxytocin have been tied to specific brain regions. Oxytocin receptors have been demonstrated in the central nucleus of the amygdala and both the anxio-lytic-like effect and the stimulation of social behavior caused by oxytocin seems to be exerted in this area. Animals that lack the gene for oxytocin loose their ability to recognize other individuals. This effect is restored by oxytocin applied locally in the amygdala (Ferguson, Aldag, Insel, & Young, 2001; Ferguson et al., 2000; Winslow et al., 2001). They also become more stressed and anxious (Amico, Mantella, Vollmer, & Li, 2004).

An important aspect of the physiology of oxytocin is that repeated administration of oxytocin induces long-lasting effects via a changed function in other transmitter systems. Five daily injections of oxytocin induce effects lasting for up to 3 weeks, including anxiolytic-like actions, lowering of blood pressure, elevation of pain thresholds, and a decrease in plasma corticosterone levels (Petersson, Ahlenius, Wiberg, Alster, & Uvnäs-Moberg, 1998a; Petersson, Alster, Lundeberg, & Uvnäs-Moberg, 1996a, 1996b; Petersson, Hulting, & Uvnäs-Moberg, 1999a), which last for 1–3 weeks after the end of the treatment. Furthermore, learning deficits due to a high stress level are markedly improved by oxytocin pretreatment, and oxytocin has also been shown to possess antidepressant-like properties in animal models (Arletti & Bertolini, 1987; (Uvnäs-Moberg, Björkstrand, Hillegaart, & Ahlenius, 1999, Uvnäs-Moberg, Eklund, Hillegaart, & Ahlenius, 2000). Finally, this treatment regimen stimulates digestion and anabolic processes, as well as weight gain, growth, and healing (Petersson, Lundeberg, Sohlström, Wiberg, & Uvnäs-Moberg, Alster, & Petersson, 1996a).

Results from neurophysiological and pharmacological experiments, as well as results from autoradiography, suggest that the long-lasting effects of oxytocin are related to adaptive changes in central neurotransmitter systems. An increased opioidergic activity lies behind the prolonged elevation of pain thresholds and an enhanced α_2-adrenoceptor function, for example, in the amygdala, hypothalamus, LC, and NTS, is related to the long term antistress-like effects (Díaz Cabiale et al., 2000; Petersson et al., 1996b; Petersson, Lundeberg, & Uvnäs-Moberg, 1999b; Petersson, Uvnäs-Moberg, Erhardt, & Engberg, 1998c). The Norepinephrine (NE) system emanating in the LC, which is strongly related to mechanisms of arousal, is inhibited by α_2-adrenoceptor activation as is the function in the sympathetic nervous system, whereas the parasympathetic tone is increased (Rajkowski, Kubiak, Ivanova, & Aston Jones, 1998). Consequently, treatment with oxytocin will result in an attenuation of arousal and stress levels. In addition, energy conservation will be stimulated. Recent data indicate that the synthesis of serotonin is increased in the frontal cortex and that cholinergic and dopaminergic transmission in the CNS may also be changed by repeated oxytocin treatment (Petersson, Hulting, Andersson, & Uvnäs-Moberg, 1999c).

Oxytocin was originally shown to be released in response to suckling during breast-feeding and in response to labor. Oxytocin is, however, also released by various types of nonnoxious stimulation (e.g., touch, warmth, and stroking) applied to all parts of the body (Ågren et al., 1995; Stock & Uvnäs-Moberg, 1988; Uvnäs-Moberg, et al., 1993) and oxytocin levels rise in plasma, cerebrospinal fluid (CSF), or both in response to these stimuli. When rats (males and females) are exposed to a stroking-like massage treatment on their chest and abdomen, oxytocin is released and an oxytocin-like effect pattern is induced. Most of these effects, including the effect on pain threshold, are blocked by an oxytocin antagonist supporting the assumption that the stroking-induced effects involve oxytocinergic transmission (Ågren et al., 1995; Lund, Lundeberg, Kurosawa, & Uvnäs-Moberg, 1999; Lund et al., 2002; Uvnäs-Moberg et al., 1996b).

Oxytocin has been shown to be released during breast-feeding in humans. Many of the psychophysiological effects of the calm and connection response occur in breast-feeding women both as an acute response and also as a more long-term adaptation. In support of a role for oxytocin in this adaptation, correlations between oxytocin levels and these effects have been demonstrated (Nissen et al., 1996; Nissen, Gustavsson, Widström, & Uvnäs-Moberg, 1998; Uvnäs-Moberg, Widström, Nissen, & Björwell, 1990; Henrichs, Neumann, & Ehlert, 2002). Oxytocin has also been shown to be released in response to sexual activity (Carmichael et al., 1987) and to massage in both sexes (Turner, Altemus, Enos, Cooper, & McGuiness, 1999). As mentioned previously, the calm and connection system is not an exclusive female type of reaction. It occurs in both men and women in response to a variety of stimuli and situations.

The authors are by no means of the opinion that oxytocin is the only mediator within the calm and connection response. Oxytocin is however unique in the sense that it may include all of the effects of the calm and connection response, cause long term effects, and is released by non-noxious sensory stimulations.

Mental Activation of the Calm and Connection Response

We have presented the idea that there is a psychophysiological system that is complementary to the fight and flight and stress responses. When this system is activated, the individual is calm and socially interactive. This state of calm and connection is induced during breast-feeding in lactating women and also by warmth and touch, for example (i.e., by somatic stimuli in individuals of any age in both sexes). We have also suggested that the peptide oxytocin via neuronal activity in the brain plays an important interactive role in

this system. Oxytocin is released from nerve terminals in brain areas involved in the control of fear, stress, and autonomic functions. The positive emotional aspects of the response such as the subjective feeling of well-being and the tendency to find the surrounding (including other individuals) as friendly and pleasant may involve a release of oxytocin in the brain (e.g., in the amygdala). In addition to acute effects, it may also induce more long-term adaptations by changing the function in other signaling systems such as the (nor)adrenergic, cholinergic, serotonergic, and opioid systems.

As mentioned previously, the fight and flight reaction may be triggered by somatic stimuli, which are related to pain or stressful situations. Any situation, however, that is experienced as dangerous, threatening, or demanding to an individual may result in defense and stress reactions, which include physiological adaptations as well as feelings of anxiety and fear. We propose by analogy that the oxytocin-related calm and connection pattern is activated by environmental factors. Thus, a calm surrounding as well as a warm, supportive, and friendly social environment may stimulate calm and social interaction. Such stimuli are likely to involve activation of oxytocin-related mechanisms. How the environmental stimuli are transmitted to the deeper limbic areas where the oxytocin system resides remains to be demonstrated. Oxytocin released (e.g., in the hypothalamus and the amygdala) may play a pivotal role by decreasing the release of CRF, which is involved in fear and stress reactions. Given the fact that repeated exposure to oxytocin induces long-term effects as described previously, sustained effects related to the calm and connection pattern may be induced in a stable, calming, friendly, and supportive environment. Such effects may at a neuroendocrine level correspond to functional adaptations of other transmitter systems as described previously and may be health promoting (Knox & Uvnäs-Moberg, 1998).

The interpretation of environmental stimuli differs between individuals, because it is dependent not only on factors such as constitution but also on previous life experiences. Memories color the interpretation of present environmental stimuli and hence the consequent reactions to these stimuli and may trigger reactions by themselves. Just as experiences of fearful situations in the past may influence the interpretation of current events, good memories may do so and make the experience of life more pleasant. Furthermore, the likelihood of friendly reactions, rather than defensive ones, is increased.

It is also of interest to mention that the release of oxytocin can be easily conditioned. Thus, a release of oxytocin and oxytocin-linked effects may be induced in a Pavlovian manner by stimuli that occur in association with a stimuli that triggers the release of oxytocin and milk ejections. Similar conditioning is likely to occur with other types of oxytocin stimuli but has not yet been shown.

Recently, Taylor demonstrated that men and women may react in different ways to stress (Taylor et al., 2002). Women are less likely than men to react with aggression and defense and instead they use and strengthen their social ties. In this context, Taylor has proposed the term "tend and befriend" for the female type of stress reaction. The calm and connection response, discussed in our article, is not a stress reaction, it is the opposite. It is an active situation related to mental calm and physical relaxation, which occurs in both women and men. However, it shares some traits with the tend-and-befriend response in the sense that it is associated with increased social interaction. The strong relationship between the function of estrogen and oxytocin may be one important factor behind the different stress reactions observed in women and men. Oxytocin can also be released in response to stress and has even been described as a stress hormone in rats but may actually serve as an endogenous stress buffering system.

It is well accepted that stressful events that occur in infancy tend to have a greater impact than those met with in adult life. Data from the field of neurobiology in rats and humans have shown that stressful experiences in early life, even *in utero,* reset the activity of the neuroendocrine systems involved in stress in such a way that stress reactions are more easily triggered in these individuals for the rest of their lives. In addition, the risk for cardiovascular and metabolic disease is increased (Barker, 1998; Sohlström, Carlsson, & Uvnäs-Moberg, 2000). Recently, using brain-imaging techniques, differences in the size of the hippocampus and amygdala have been demonstrated in adults who were exposed to abuse during childhood. These permanent anatomical changes in the brain may be related to the high levels of anxiety and fearfulness often observed in these individuals (Teicher, 2002).

However, experiences from early life may also influence the individual in a positive direction. Experiments demonstrate that rats exposed to extra oxytocin as newborns have lower activity in their HPA axes and lower blood pressure as adults (Holst, Petersson, & Uvnäs-Moberg, 2002). Furthermore, functional changes have been demonstrated in the amygdala, which plays such a decisive role in emotionality. Rats exposed to high amounts of maternal interaction during the 1st week of life have been shown to have more oxytocin receptors in the amygdala as adults and also to be less anxious and also more interactive to their own offspring (Caldij, Diorio, & Meaney, 2000; Champagne & Meaney, 2001). Because the human brain also has been shown to be extremely open for external stimulation and information early in life, individuals who have been exposed to a warm and caring childhood might have a more trusting friendly attitude toward the surrounding, possibly because their brains

were more influenced by oxytocin (or by other neuroendocrine mechanisms with similar effect patterns) early in life.

The Process of Socialization

Socialized individuals are defined as those who are cognizant of and have integrated social and cultural norms and values, apply those norms and values when confronted with dilemmas, and are respectful of the right of others. Darwin (1873) proposed that socialization of humankind and the development of emotions and social behavior consistent with protecting of others has an adaptive and evolutionary value. At an individual level, the socialized person takes the perspective of others into consideration in interpersonal exchanges and does no harm to others. It is tempting to suggest that an adequate stimulation of the calm and connection system during early life is of utmost importance for the establishment of the brain and related biological structures that can form the platform for the development of a socialized individual, given a certain biological disposition.

Comments

The human individual functions and develops as an integrated psychological, biological, and social being. Understanding individual functioning and development from a holistic, or organismic perspective as the biologists prefer to call it, requires a general model of the human being. This is a prerequisite for the synthesis of knowledge that can contribute to the understanding of individual mental, behavioral, biological, and social activities (Magnusson, 2001). From this perspective, the discussion here of the calm and connection system serves to fill in a vacant space in the model of the psychobiological system.

As an integrated part of the functioning of the total organism, the concept of a calm and connection system enriches the theoretical basis for empirical research in the recently developed area that has been designated "positive development" (e.g., Cowen, 1991; Ryff & Singer, 1998). As was argued by Magnusson and Mahoney (2002), successful research in that area requires a holistic, interactionistic frame of reference to enable the formulation of the necessary synthesis of knowledge.

As was emphasized in the introduction, a central role in the holistic integration of the fight–flight and stress system, on the one hand, and the calm–connection system, on the other, is played by the brain. During infancy, the brain is particularly open for and dependent on stimulation from the social and physical environment. Under optimal conditions, the individual brain develops in such a way that adequate positive and negative emotions are attached to the information offered by the environment as well as to conscious and unconscious mental activities. According to the holistic view, in this developmental process the calm and connection system is also involved. It is a requirement for the socialization of the individual that the developmental process in this respect proceeds in an optimal way.

References

Ågren, G., Lundeberg, T., Uvnäs-Moberg, K., & Sato, A. (1995). The oxytocin antagonist 1-deamino–2-D-Tyr-(Oet)–4-Thr–8-Orn-oxytocin reverses the increase in the withdrawal response latency to thermal, but not mechanical nociceptive stimuli following oxytocin administration or massage-like stroking in rats. *Neuroscience Letters, 187,* 49–52.

Amico, J. A., Mantella, R. C., Vollmer, R. R., & Li, X. (2004). Anxiety and stress responses in female oxytocin deficient mice. *J Neuroendocrinology, 16,* 319–324.

Arletti, R., & Bertolini, A. (1987). Oxytocin as an antidepressant in two animal models of depression. *Life Sciences, 41,* 1725–1730.

Barker, D. J. P. (1998). In utero programming of chronic disease. *Clinical Science, 95,* 115–128.

Caldij, C., Diorio, J., & Meaney, M. J. (2000). Variations in maternal care in infancy regulate the development of stress reactivity. *Biological Psychiatry, 15,* 1164–1174

Cannon, W. B. (1929). *Bodily changes in pain, hunger, fear and rage.* New York: Appleton.

Carmichael, M. S., Humbert, R., Dixen, J., Palmisano, G., Greenleaf, W., & Davidson, J. M. (1987). Plasma oxytocin increases in the human sexual response. *Journal of Clinical Endocrinology and Metabolism, 64,* 27–31.

Carter, C. S. (1998). Neuroendocrine perspectives on social attachment and love. *Psychoneuroendocrinology, 23,* 779–818.

Champagne, F., & Meaney, M. J. (2001). Like mother, like daughter. Evidence for nongenomic transmission of parental behavior and stress responsivity. *Progress in Brain Research, 133,* 287–302.

Choleris, E., Gustafsson, J. A., Korach, K. S., Muglia, L. J., Pfaff, D. W., & Ogawa, S. (2003). An estrogen-dependent four-gene micronet regulating social recognition: A study with oxytocin and estrogoen receptor-alpha and-beta knockout mice. *Proceedings of the National Academy of Science, 13,* 6192–7.

Chrousos, G. P., & Gold, P. W. (1992). The concepts of stress and stress system disorders. Overview of physical and behavioral homeostasis. *Journal of the American Medical Association, 267,* 1244–1252.

Cowen, E. L. (1991). In pursuit of wellness. *American Psychologist, 46,* 404–408.

Darwin, C. (1873). *The expression of emotions in man and animals.* New York: Appleton.

Díaz-Cabiale, Z., Petersson, M., Narváez, J. A., Uvnäs-Moberg, K., & Fuxe, K. (2000). Systemic oxytocin treatment modulates alpha2/adrenoceptors in telencephalic and diencephalic regions of the rat. *Brain Research, 887,* 421–425.

Ferguson, J. N., Aldag, J. M., Insel, T. R., & Young, L. J. (2001). Oxytocin in the medial amygdala is essential for social recognition in the mouse. *Journal of Neuroscience, 158,* 278–285.

Ferguson, J. N., Young, L. J., Harn, E. F., Nazuk, M. M., Insel, T. R., & Winslow, J. T. (2000). Social amnesia in mice lacking the oxytocin gene. *Nature Genetics, 25,* 284–288.

Heinrichs, M., Neumann, I., & Ehlert, U. (2002). Lactation and stress: Protective effects of breastfeeding in humans. *Stress, 5,* 195–203.

Insel, T. R. (1992). Oxytocin—A neuropeptide for affiliation: Evidence from behavioral, receptor autoradiographic and comparative studies. *Psychoneuroendocrinology, 17,* 3–35.

Holst, S., Uvnäs-Moberg, K., & Petersson, M. (2000). Postnatal oxytocin treatment and postnatal stroking of rats reduce blood pressure in adulthood. *Autonomic Neuroscience, 30,* 85–90.

Kendrick, K. M., Keverne, E. B., Baldwin, B. A., & Sharman, D. F. (1986). Cerebrospinal fluid levels of acetylcholinesterase, monoamines and oxytocin during labour, parturition, vaginocervical stimulation, lamb separation and suckling in sheep. *Neuroendocrinology, 44,* 149–156.

Knox, S. S., & Uvnäs-Moberg, K. (1998). Social isolation and cardiovascular disease: An atherosclerotic pathway? *Psychoneuroendocrinology, 23,* 877–890.

Lund, I., Lundeberg, T., Kurosawa, M., & Uvnäs-Moberg, K. (1999). Sensory stimulation (massage) reduces blood pressure in unanaesthetized rats. *Journal of the Autonomic Nervous System, 78,* 30–37.

Lund, I., Yu, L. C., Uvnäs-Moberg, K., Wang, J., Yu, C., Kurosawa, M., Ågren, G., Rosen, A., Lekman, M., & Lundeberg, T. (2002). Repeated massage-like stimulation induces long-term effects on nociception: Contribution of oxytocinergic mechanisms. *European Journal of Neuroscience, 16,* 330–338.

Magnusson, D. (2001). The holistic-interactionistic paradigm: Some directions for empirical developmental research. *European Psychologist, 6,* 153–162.

Magnusson, D. (2003). The person approach: Concepts, measurement models, and research strategies. *New Directions in Child Development* (Special issue), *101,* 3–23.

Magnusson, D., & Mahoney, J. L. (2002). A holistic person approach for research on positive development. In G. Aspinwall & U. M. Staudinger (Eds.), *A psychology of human strengths: Fundamental questions and future directions for a positive psychology* (pp. 227–243). Washington, DC: American Psychological Association.

Mason, J. W. (1968a). A review of psychoendocrine research on the sympathetic-adrenal medullary system. *Psychosomatic Medicine, 30,* 631–653.

Mason, J. W. (1968b). A review of psychoendocrine research on the pituitary-adrenal cortical system. *Psychosomatic Medicine, 30,* 567–597.

McCarthy, M. M., & Altemus, M. (1997). Central nervous system actions of oxytocin and modulation of behavior in humans. *Molecular Medicine Today, 3,* 269–275.

Nissen, E., Gustavsson, P., Widström, A. M., & Uvnäs-Moberg, K. (1998). Oxytocin, prolactin, milk production and their relationship with personality traits in women after vaginal delivery or cesarean section. *Journal of Psychosomatic Obstetrics and Gynaecology, 19,* 49–58.

Nissen, E., Uvnäs-Moberg, K., Svensson, K., Stock, S., Widström, A. M., & Winberg, J. (1996). Different patterns of oxytocin, prolactin but not cortisol release during breastfeeding in women delivered by caesarean section or by the vaginal route. *Early Human Development, 45,* 103–118.

Petersson, M., Ahlenius, S., Wiberg, U., Alster, P., & Uvnäs-Moberg, K. (1998a). Steroid dependent effects of oxytocin on spontaneous motor activity in female rats. *Brain Research Bulletin, 45,* 301–305.

Petersson, M., Alster, P., Lundeberg, T., & Uvnäs-Moberg, K. (1996a). Oxytocin causes a long-term decrease of blood pressure in female and male rats. *Physiology & Behavior, 60,* 1311–1315.

Petersson, M., Alster, P., Lundeberg, T., & Uvnäs-Moberg, K. (1996b). Oxytocin increases nociceptive thresholds in a long-term perspective in female and male rats. *Neuroscience Letters, 212,* 87–90.

Petersson, M., Hulting, A. L., Andersson, R., & Uvnäs-Moberg, K. (1999c). Long-term changes in gastrin, cholecystokinin and insulin in response to oxytocin treatment. *Neuroendocrinology, 69,* 202–208.

Petersson, M., Hulting, A.-L., & Uvnäs-Moberg, K. (1999a). Oxytocin causes a sustained decrease in plasma levels of corticosterone in rats. *Neuroscience Letters, 264,* 41–44.

Petersson, M., Lundeberg, T., Sohlström, A., Wiberg, U., & Uvnäs-Moberg, K. (1998b). Oxytocin increases the survival of musculocutaneous flaps. *Naunyn-Schmiedeberg's Archives of Pharmacology, 357,* 701–704.

Petersson, M., Lundeberg, T., & Uvnäs-Moberg, K. (1999b). Oxytocin enhances the effects of clonidine on blood pressure and locomotor activity in rats. *Journal of the Autonomic Nervous System, 78,* 49–56.

Petersson, M., Uvnäs-Moberg, K., Erhardt, S., & Engberg, G. (1998c). Oxytocin increases locus coeruleus alpha 2-adrenoceptor responsiveness in rats. *Neuroscience Letters, 255,* 115–118.

Rajkowski, J., Kubiak, P., Ivanova, S., & Aston Jones, G. (1998). State related activity, reactivity of locus coeruleus neurons in behaving monkeys. In D. Goldstein, G. Eisenhofer, & T. McCarty (Eds.), *Advances in pharmacology, catecholamines bridging basic science with clinical medicine* (pp. 740–744). San Diego, CA: Academic.

Richard, P., Moos, F., & Freund-Mercier, M.-J. (1991). Central effects of oxytocin. *Physiology Review, 71,* 331–370.

Ryff, C. D., & Singer, B. (1998). The contours of positive human health. *Psychological Inquiry, 9,* 1–28.

Sansone, G. R., Gerdes, C. A., Steinman, J. L., Winslow, J. T., Ottenweller, J. E., Komisaruk, B. R., & Insel, T. R. (2002). Vaginocervical stimulation releases oxytocin within the spinal cord in rats. *Neuroendocrinology, 75,* 306–315.

Selye, H. (1976). *Stress in health and disease.* Boston: Butterworths.

Sofroniew, M. W. (1983). Vasopressin and oxytocin in the mammalian brain and spinal cord. *Trends in Neuroscience, 6,* 467–472.

Sohlstöm, A., Carlsson, C., & Uvnäs-Moberg, K. (2000). Effects of oxytocin treatment in early life on body weight and corticosterone in adult offspring from ad libitum fed and food restricted rats. *Biology of the Neonate, 78,* 33–40.

Stock, S., & Uvnäs-Moberg, K. (1988). Increased plasma levels of oxytocin in response to afferent electrical stimulation of the sciatic and vagal nerves and in response to touch and pinch in anaesthetized rats. *Acta Physiologica Scandinavica, 132,* 29–34.

Taylor, S. E., Klein, L. C., Gruenewald, T. L., Gurung, R. A., & Updegraffe, J. A. (2002). Biobehavioural responses to stress in females: Tend and befriend, not fight-flight. *Psychological Review, 107,* 411–429.

Teicher, M. H. (2002, March). Scars that won't heal: The neurobiology of child abuse. *Scientific American, 286,* 54–61.

Turner, R. A., Altemus, M., Enos, T., Cooper, B., & McGuiness, T. (1999). Preliminary research on plasma oxytocin in normal cycling women: Investigating emotion and interpersonal distress. *Psychiatry, 62,* 97–113.

Uvnäs-Moberg, K. (1997). Oxytocin-linked antistress effects—the relaxation and growth response. *Acta Physiologica Scandinavica, 161*(Suppl. 640), 38–42.

Uvnäs-Moberg, K. (1998a). Antistress pattern induced by oxytocin. *News in Physiological Sciences, 13,* 22–26.

Uvnäs-Moberg, K. (1998b). Oxytocin may mediate the benefits of positive social interaction and emotions. *Psychoneuroendocrinology, 23,* 819–825.

Uvnäs-Moberg, K. (2003). *The oxytocin factor: Tapping the hormone of calm, love and healing.* Boston: Perseus.

Uvnäs-Moberg, K., Ahlenius, S., Hillegaart, V., & Alster, P. (1994). High doses of oxytocin cause sedation and low doses cause an anxiolytic-like effect in male rats. *Pharmacology, Biochemistry, and Behavior, 49,* 101–106.

Uvnäs-Moberg, K., Alster, P., Hillegaart, V., & Ahlenius, S. (1992). Oxytocin reduces exploratory motor behavior and shifts the activity towards the centre of the arena in male rats. *Acta Physiologica Scandinavica, 145,* 429–430.

Uvnäs-Moberg, K., Alster, P., & Petersson, M. (1996a). Dissociation of oxytocin effects on body weight on two variants of female Sprague-Dawley rats. *Integrative Physiological and Behavioral Science, 31,* 44–55.

Uvnäs-Moberg, K., Alster, P., Lund, I., Lundeberg, T., Kurosawa, M., & Ahlenius, S. (1996b). Stroking of the abdomen causes decreased locomotor activity in conscious male rats. *Physiology & Behavior, 60,* 1409–1411.

Uvnäs-Moberg, K., Björkstrand, E., Hillegaart, V., & Ahlenius, S. (1999). Oxytocin as a possible mediator of SSRI-induced antidepressant effects. *Psychopharmacology. 142,* 95–101.

Uvnäs-Moberg, K., Bruzelius, G., Alster, P., & Lundeberg, T. (1993). The antinociceptive effect of non-noxious sensory stimulation is mediated partly through oxytocinergic mechanisms. *Acta Physiologica Scandinavica, 149,* 199–204.

Uvnäs-Moberg, K., Eklund, M., Hillegaart, V., & Ahlenius, S. (2000). Improved conditioned avoidance learning by oxytocin administration in high-emotional male Sprague-Dawley rats. *Regulatory Peptides, 88,* 27–32.

Uvnäs-Moberg, K., Widström, A. M., Nissen, E., & Björwell, H. (1990). Personality traits in women 4 days postpartum and their correlation with plasma levels of oxytocin and prolactin. *Journal of Psychosomatic Obstetrics and Gynaecology, 11,* 261–273.

Wigger, A., & Neumann, I. D. (2002). Endogenous opioid regulation of stress-induced oxytocin release within the hypothalamic paraventricular nucleus is reversed in late pregnancy: A microdialysis study. *Neuroscience, 112,* 121–9.

Windle, R. J., Shanks, N., Lightman, S. L., & Ingram, C. D. (1997). Central oxytocin administration reduces stress-induced corticosterone release and anxiety behavior in rats. *Endocrinology, 138,* 2829–2834.

Winslow, J. T., Hearn, E. F., Fergusson, J., Young, L. J., Matzuk, M. M., & Insel, T. R. (2001). Infant vocalization, adult aggression and fear behavior of an oxytocin null mutant mouse. *Hormones and Behavior, 39,* 11–21.

International Journal of Behavioral Medicine
2005, Vol. 12, No. 2, 66–77

Altruism, Happiness, and Health: It's Good to Be Good

Stephen G. Post

Altruistic (other-regarding) emotions and behaviors are associated with greater well-being, health, and longevity. This article presents a summary and assessment of existing research data on altruism and its relation to mental and physical health. It suggests several complimentary interpretive frameworks, including evolutionary biology, physiological models, and positive psychology. Potential public health implications of this research are discussed, as well as directions for future studies. The article concludes, with some caveats, that a strong correlation exists between the well-being, happiness, health, and longevity of people who are emotionally and behaviorally compassionate, so long as they are not overwhelmed by helping tasks.

Key words: kindness, altruism, well-being, happiness, health, public health

The vast majority of people in the European Union and the United States have more material wealth than did their parents; the percentage of these populations that is happy, however, has not increased, and depression and anxiety rates have risen dramatically (Easterbrook, 2003). The rise in depression rates is in part due to greater public and medical awareness. However, such elevated rates require serious reflection on our social environment, which has been described by one sociologist with the terms "bowling alone" and loss of "social capital" (Putnam, 2001). These terms suggest that a partial solution to the problem may lie with the restoration of prosocial altruistic emotions and behaviors. Current research does indeed show a strong association between kindly emotions, helping behavior, or both, on the one hand, and well-being, health, and longevity, on the other. This article summarizes and interprets existing research, points to future research directions, and suggests implications of such research for public health.

If kind emotions, helping behavior, or both are associated with well-being, health, and longevity, the implications for how we think about human nature and prosperity are significant (Hendrick & Hendrick, 1986; Levin, 2000). Although those who are physically overwhelmed, mentally overwhelmed, or both by the needs of others do experience a stressful "burden" that can have significant negative health consequences, as in the case of the stressed caregiver of a loved one with dementia (Kiecolt-Glaser, Preacher, MacCallum, Malarkey, & Glaser, 2003), there are health benefits linked to helping behavior when it is not experienced as overwhelming. A relevant study (Schwartz, Meisenhelder, Ma, & Reed, 2003) points to health benefits in generous behavior but with the important caveat that there are clear adverse health consequences associated with being overly taxed. Although the health benefits of receiving love are widely deemed significant, we want to go beyond the recipient to examine benefits for the agent. What happens to the health and longevity of people who are (a) emotionally kind, (b) charitable in their actions toward others without being overwhelmed, or both?

Emotional states and related behaviors have been studied by mainstream scientists in relation to health promotion and disease prevention (Oman, Thoresen, & McMahon, 1999; Young & Glasgow, 1998). However, the impact of positive emotional states and related behaviors on health constitutes a novel area for researchers (Edwards & Cooper, 1988). In the 1990s, for example, Danner et al. (2001) reviewed short, personal essays written by nuns in the 1930s; this was a secondary project in their famous nun study on Alzheimer disease. The nuns who expressed the most positive emotions were living about 10 years longer than those who expressed the fewest such emotions, and they were somewhat protected from the onset of dementia (Danner et al., 2001). In another example, Fredrickson (2003) summarized 2 decades of investigation and concluded that positive emotions were linked with a "broader thought-action repertoire," which is to say that "big picture" creative thinking was enhanced (as measured by standard tests). Drawing on her own studies and those of Alice Isen (1987), Fredrickson found that "when people feel good, their thinking becomes more creative, integrative, flexible and open to information" (p. 333). She

Stephen G. Post, Department of Bioethics, School of Medicine, Case Western Reserve University, Cleveland, Ohio 44106–4976, USA.

The author wishes to acknowledge the support of the John Templeton Foundation; the Institute for Research on Unlimited Love—Altruism, Compassion, Service; and the Ford Foundation.

Correspondence concerning this article should be addressed to Stephen G. Post, Department of Bioethics, School of Medicine, Case Western Reserve University, Cleveland, Ohio 44106–4976, USA. E-mail: sgp2@cwru.edu also found that positive emotions enhanced psychological and physical resilience and interpreted this effect as a result of the "undoing" of negative emotions that are clearly physically harmful. However, "helpful compassionate acts," she also argued, just allow people to feel elevated and good about themselves and others (Post, Underwood, Schloss, & Hurlbut, 2002).

There are few new ideas in the world. The link between "reasonable" altruism—that is, helping behavior that is not overwhelming—and health is at the core of Dickens' story of Ebenezer Scrooge; for with each new expression of benevolence, Scrooge became more buoyant, until finally he was among the most generous of men in all of England and appeared all the more effervescent and fit. He surely felt a great deal happier with life the more generous he became, following the pattern of the "helper's high" (Luks, 1988). There is no either–or dualism between quickening that innate capacity for benevolence and the fuller actualization of a happier and healthier self (Frankl, 1956). Setting aside preoccupation with "purity" and perfectly selfless motives, it may be that people who live generous lives soon become aware that in the giving of self lies the unsought discovery of self as the old selfish pursuit of happiness is subjectively revealed as futile and shortsighted. Dostoyevsky's images of the Elder Zossima have the same buoyancy. Jewish, Hindu, Buddhist, Islamic, and Native American spiritual traditions highlight the flourishing that follows from a life of unselfish love—a life in tune with one's true self (Post, 2002). Thus, there is an alternative image to that of the selfless ascetic who seems intent on withering away, (Goode, 1959).

Scientifically speaking, however, is a generous and loving life typically happier, healthier, and longer than a life of negative affect and solipsism? Is it unhealthy to feel and behave as though one is the center of the universe, relating to others only in so far as they contribute to "my" agendas? The link between altruism and health is important to how we think of human nature and human fulfillment, and it was alluded to a half century ago. Sorokin (1954/2002), in his classic 1954 treatise entitled *The Ways and Power of Love,* began his "Preface" with the assertion that unselfish love and altruism are "necessary for physical, mental, and moral health" and that "altruistic persons live longer than egoistic individuals" (p. xi). Although he did not make a clear scientific case to demonstrate a link between altruism and prolongevity, he did use available historical collections of the lives of the saints to argue that such generous people generally live longer—unless their lives are cut short by misfortune. Erik Erikson, another maverick Harvard professor at the time, lightly surmised a connection between health and generativity—that is, altruism in older adults focused on a younger generational cohort. This connection is currently being examined

in a major longitudinal prospective study of Harvard graduates over a 50-year period (Vaillant, 2002).

It is already well established that compassion, love, and social support have health benefits for recipients (Ainsworth et al., 1978; Harlow, 1958). Researchers in the late 1970s, for example, were studying the effects of a diet high in fat and cholesterol in rabbits. One subgroup of rabbits had 60% less atherosclerosis than the group as a whole, even though they ate the same diet. The only notable difference in treatment was that the healthier subgroup was fed and cared for by a lab assistant who took them out of their cages, petted them, and talked to them before feeding. The study was repeated twice with the same results and was reported in *Science* (Nerem, Levesque, & Cornhill, 1980). Also in this early period, researchers followed 10,000 Israeli men aged 40 years and older to clarify the risk factors for angina pectoris. Anxiety and severe psychosocial problems were confirmed risks; in addition, "those who perceived their wives to be loving and supportive had half the rate of angina of those who felt unloved and unsupported" (Medalie & Goldbourt, 1976, p. 917). A wife's love was later associated with lowered risk of duodenal ulcers (Medalie, Stange, Zyzanski, & Goldbourt, 1992). Studies show depressed lymphocyte function after bereavement (Bartrop, Lazarus, Luckhurst, Kiloh, & Penny, 1977). When love is lost due to the death of a beloved spouse, T and B cells in the immune system behave abnormally and, for many months, must be stimulated to perform their usual functions (Rees & Lutkins, 1967, Zisook, 1987). In a remarkable study that needs to be replicated, 126 healthy young men were randomly selected in the early 1950s from the Harvard classes of 1952 and 1954 and given questionnaires about their perceptions of the love they felt from their parents. Thirty-five years later, 91% of participants who did not perceive themselves to have had warm relationships with their mothers had diagnosed midlife diseases (coronary artery disease, high blood pressure, duodenal ulcer, and alcoholism), as compared to only 45% of those who reported a warm relationship with their mothers; 82% of those indicated low warmth and closeness to their fathers had such diagnoses, compared with 50% who reported high warmth and closeness. One hundred percent of those who reported low warmth and closeness from both parents had diseases diagnosed in midlife, whereas only 47% who reported both parents as being warm and close had midlife diagnoses (Russek & Schwartz, 1997). Although this Harvard study needs corroboration, it points to the now widely accepted biopsychosocial model that being loved, cared for, and supported by others is critically important to health and treatment efficacy (Goodkin & Visser, 2000). No one questions the importance to health of *receiving* compassionate love (Ornish, 1999). However, this end of the spectrum needs to be balanced with a focus on the importance to health of *giving* unselfish love.

Biogerontologists are studying the molecular and cellular science of aging with the goal of its eventual deceleration (Post & Binstock, 2004). One plausible hypothesis that should be simultaneously investigated is longevity enhancement through the cultivation of generous emotions and helping behaviors. On the one hand, it is intriguing to see that genetic modifications of fruit flies and nematode worms, caloric restriction in mice and primates, and related antioxidant studies all point toward the possibility in future decades of longer human lives through biotechnology (Post & Binstock, 2004). However, this technological approach does not ensure that longer lives will be morally good lives, whereas the inner cultivation of altruistic and loving emotions coupled with generous actions does (Post, 2004). A new direction in the emotional and behavioral aspects of antiaging research (Epel et al., 2004) indicates that chronic stress impacts health by modulating the rate of cellular aging. Evidence is mounting that psychological stress is associated with higher oxidative stress, lower telomerase activity, and shorter telomere length, all of which are known determinants of cell senescence and longevity. In this study, women with the highest levels of perceived stress had telomeres that were, on average, shortened by 1 decade when compared with low-stress women. Thus, stress accelerates aging and increases susceptibility to the many illnesses for which age is the major risk factor (Epel et al., 2004).

Cultivating loving emotions, engaging in helping and self-forgetful activities, and a serene spirituality may thus contribute to good health and longevity by preventing the acceleration of aging at the cellular level. In commenting on this study, Sapolsky (2004) indicates that, although more research is needed, the Epel et al. (2004) study points to a pathway by which stress influences a fundamental aspect of the aging process.

What do we really know, scientifically, about altruism, happiness, and health? (Rotzein et al., 1994). Evidence has been accumulating for several decades, and research has clearly escalated since the late 1990s.

Background of Existing Research

This section presents a brief overview of existing studies on altruism that are relevant to mental and physical health.

Mental Health

Well-being consists of feeling hopeful, happy, and good about oneself, as well as energetic and connected to others. An early study compared retirees older than the age 65 who volunteered with those who did not (Hunter & Lin, 1980–1981). Volunteers scored significantly higher in life satisfaction and will to live and had fewer symptoms of depression, anxiety, and somatization. Because there were no differences in demographic and other background variables between the groups, the researchers concluded that volunteer activity helped explain these mental health benefits. The nonvolunteers did spend more days in the hospital and were taking more medications, which may have prevented them from volunteering. However, the mental health benefits persisted after controlling for disability. In another older study, families of recently deceased loved ones reported a psychological benefit from their decision to donate organs (Batten & Prottas, 1987). More recent studies confirm an association between altruistic activities and both well-being and life satisfaction in older adults (Dulin & Hill, 2003; Liang, Krause, & Bennett, 2001; Morrow-Howell, Hinterlonh, Rozario, & Tang, 2003).

Midlarsky (1991) posed five reasons for benefits to older adults who engage in altruistic behavior: enhanced social integration, distraction from the agent's own problems, enhanced meaningfulness, increased perception of self-efficacy and competence, and improved mood or more physically active lifestyle. Midlarsky and Kahana (1994) associated adult altruism—that is, voluntary behavior that is "motivated by concern for the welfare of the other, rather than by anticipation of rewards" (p. 11)—with improved morale, self-esteem, positive affect, and well-being.

The mental health benefits of volunteerism include reduction in depressive symptoms (Musick & Wilson, 2003), happiness, and enhanced well-being (Krueger, Hicks, & McGue, 2001). Schwartz et al. (2003) focused on a stratified random sample of 2,016 members of the Presbyterian Church located throughout the United States. The study's purpose was to investigate whether altruistic social behaviors such as helping others were associated with better physical and mental health. Mailed questionnaires evaluated giving and receiving help, prayer activities, positive and negative religious coping, and self-reported physical and mental health. Multivariate regression analysis revealed no association between giving or receiving help and physical functioning, although the sample was skewed toward high physical functioning. After adjusting for age, gender, stressful life events, income, general health, religious coping, and asking God for healing, both helping others and receiving help were associated with mental health (i.e., anxiety and depression). *Giving help was more significantly associated with better mental health than was receiving help.* The authors concluded that "helping others is associated with higher levels of mental health, above and beyond the benefits of receiving help and other known psychospiritual, stress, and demographic factors" (p. 782). The authors also add an important caveat that "feeling overwhelmed by others' demands had a stronger negative relationship with mental health than helping others had a positive one" (p. 783). (Whether some forms of helping are more rewarding than others is not examined.)

Physical Health

A review of existing studies indicates that research on the effect of kindness and volunteerism on health may have begun inadvertently in 1956, when a team of researchers from Cornell University School of Medicine began following 427 married women with children under the hypothesis that housewives with more children would be under greater stress and die earlier than women with few children (Moen, Dempster-McCain, & Williams, 1993). Surprisingly, they found that numbers of children, education, class, and work status did not affect longevity. After following these women for 30 years, however, it was found that 52% of those who did not belong to a volunteer organization had experienced a major illness, compared to 36% who did belong. Although a potential confounding factor is that people who volunteer may start out in better physical health, this would not greatly diminish the study's implications.

A study by Musick, Herzog, and House (1999) examined the hypothesis that older volunteers benefit in terms of health as well as well-being. Based on data from a nationally representative sample, the study used Cox proportional hazards regression to estimate the effects of volunteering on the rate of mortality among persons 65 and older. The data are a multistage stratified area sample representative of the noninstitutionalized U.S. population aged 25 and older; the response rate was 67% of sampled individuals and 68% for sampled households. The data were collected over three waves: 1986 ($n = 3,617$), 1989 ($n = 2,867$), 1994 ($n = 2,348$). Face-to-face interviews were conducted in the respondents' homes. From mid-1986 through March 1994, deaths were ascertained through tracking and interview processes and via the National Death Index. Respondents were asked whether they had volunteered in the past year through a religious, educational, political, senior citizen, or other organization. Respondents who had volunteered were asked how much time they had devoted to volunteerism. Controlled analysis indicated that the protective effects of volunteering "were strongest among those volunteering for one organization or for less than forty hours" (Musick et al., 1999, p. S175) and among those who lacked other social supports. Moderate amounts of volunteerism were associated with lowered risk of death. Indeed, simply adding the volunteering role was protective (Musick et al., 1999). One need not volunteer to a great extent to

have benefits, and too much volunteering to the point of strain "incurs just enough detriments to offset the potential beneficial effects of the activity" (Musick et al., 1999, S178). The researchers added that 69% who reported volunteering did so through a religious organization, but they found no relation between reduced risk of mortality and religious service attendance. Volunteering, rather than its religious context, explained the effect.

Oman of the University of California at Berkeley is one of the leading researchers in this field. Oman et al. (1999) focused on 2,025 community-dwelling residents of Marin County, California, who were first examined in 1990–1991. All respondents were 55 or older at this baseline examination; 95% were non-Hispanic White, 58% were women, and a majority had annual incomes above $15,000. Residents were classified as practicing "high volunteerism" if they were involved in two or more helping organizations and as practicing "moderate volunteerism" if they were involved in one. The number of hours invested in helping behavior was also measured, although this was not as predictive as the number of organizations. Physical health status was assessed on the basis of reported medical diagnoses, as well as such factors as "tiring easily" and self-perceived overall health. Thirty-one percent ($n = 630$) of these elderly participants participated in some kind of volunteer activity, and about half volunteered for more than one organization. Those who volunteered for two or more organizations experienced a 63% lower likelihood of dying during the study period than did nonvolunteers. Even after controlling for age, gender, number of chronic conditions, physical mobility, exercise, self-rated general health, health habits (smoking), social support (marital status, religious attendance), and psychological status (depressive symptoms), this effect was only reduced to a still highly significant 44%.

Observational physical performance measures and self-reported functioning measures were included. Sociodemographic data were collected, as well as information on social functioning and support. Frequency of attendance at religious services was included in the many social functioning questions. Psychological measures were implemented as well. Mortality was determined by screening local newspapers, attempted contact for reinterview at the time of a second interview, and submission of names to the National Death Index. Mortality was examined from 1990 through November 13, 1995, the closing date of the second examination. During this follow-up period of 3.2 to 5.6 years, 203 (23.8%) men and 247 (21.1%) women died. Remarkably, "the mortality rate of 30.1 among nonvolunteers declined by 26 percent to 24.2 ($p = .04$) among moderate volunteers, and by an *additional* 50 percent to 12.8 ($p = .008$) among high volunteers (two or more organizations)" (Oman et al., 1999, p. 307).

Multivariate adjusted associations indicated that moderate volunteerism was not statistically significant after controlling for health status. High volunteerism remained significantly associated with lower mortality rates. Specifically, "the 44 percent reduction in mortality associated with high volunteerism in this study was larger than the reductions associated with physical mobility (39 percent), exercising four times weekly (30 percent), and weekly attendance at religious services (29 percent), and was only slightly smaller than the reduction associated with not smoking (49 percent)" (Oman et al., 1999, p. 310; Oman & Reed, 1998).

On a cross-cultural level, Krause, Ingersoll-Dayton, Liang, and Sugisawa (1999) at the University of Michigan studied a sample of 2,153 older adults in Japan, examining the relations among religion, providing help to others, and health. They found that those who provided more assistance to others were significantly more likely to indicate that their physical health was better. The authors concluded that the relation between religion and better health could be at least partly explained by the increased likelihood of religious persons helping others.

The benefits of altruism are not limited to older adults (Omato & Snyder, 1995); the differences in health outcomes between helpers and nonhelpers is more difficult to detect in younger age groups, however, where health is not affected by susceptibilities associated with aging (House et al., 1982). Ironson, Solomon, and Balbin (2002) at the University of Miami compared the characteristics of long-term survivors with AIDS ($n = 79$) with a HIV-positive comparison group equivalent (based on CD4 count) that had been diagnosed for a relatively shorter time ($n = 200$). These investigators found that survivors were significantly more likely to be spiritual or religious. The effect of spirituality and religiousness on survival, however, was mediated by "helping others with HIV." Thus, helping others (altruism) accounted for a significant part of the relation between spirituality and religiousness and long-term survival in this study.

Brown et al. (2003) reported on a 5-year study involving 423 older couples. Each couple was asked what type of practical support they provided for friends or relatives, if they could count on help from others when needed, and what type of emotional support they gave each other. A total of 134 people died over the 5 years. After adjusting for a variety of factors—including age, gender, and physical and emotional health—the researchers found an association between reduced risk of dying and giving help but no association between receiving help and reduced death risk. Brown, a researcher at the University of Michigan's Institute for Social Research, concluded that those who provided no instrumental or emotional support to others were more than twice as likely to die in the 5 years as people who helped spouses, friends, relatives, and neighbors.

Despite concerns that the longevity effects might be due to a healthier individual's greater ability to provide help, the results remained the same after the researchers controlled for functional health, health satisfaction, health behaviors, age, income, education level, and other possible confounders. The researchers concluded that "If giving, rather than receiving, promotes longevity, then interventions that are currently designed to help people feel supported may need to be redesigned so that the emphasis is on what people do to help others" (Brown, Nesse, Vonokur, & Smith, 2003, p. 326).

The Plausibility of Altruistic Causality

Altruism results in deeper and more positive social integration, distraction from personal problems and the anxiety of self-preoccupation, enhanced meaning and purpose as related to well-being, a more active lifestyle that counters cultural pressures toward isolated passivity, and the presence of positive emotions such as kindness that displace harmful negative emotional states. It is entirely plausible, then, to assert that altruism enhances mental and physical health.

It must always be kept in mind that significant findings regarding health in relation to altruism and other phenomena in population studies are expressed (a) on average, (b) across a given population, and (c) all things being equal. In other words, what we can conclude, at best, is that altruism is one of the factors that increases the odds of well-being, better health, or survival in many people; it is no guarantee of good health. This could be said of any ostensible protective factors—for example, good diet, low blood pressure, not smoking, good family history, not living in poverty, nontoxic environment, and educational level.

Studies using biological markers provide a stronger basis for claiming that altruistic emotions and behaviors *cause* better mental or physical health. If someone is depressed or physically disabled, it is less likely that he or she will engage in helping behaviors. In this sense, there is a selection of the healthy into altruism, and this partially explains the better health of altruists. However, there is more to this story. Other-regarding behavior orders and shapes the lives of individuals in profound ways that improves their health and lengthens their lives. People engaged in helping behavior do generally report feeling good about themselves, and this has measurable physiological correlates. Studies using biological markers look at individuals before and after engagement in altruistic moods and behaviors and indicate immune-enhancing biological changes (see the section on physiological advantages).

The argument for causality is further strengthened by the inarguable assertion that emotional states of unselfish love and kindness displace negative emotional states (e.g., rage, hatred, fear), which cause stress and stress-related illness through adverse impact on immune function (Fredrickson, 2003; Lawler et al., 2003; Sternberg, 2001). Thus, the cultivation of other-regarding affections eliminates negative emotional states that are often harmful to health.

Although it is the case that people who are altruistic must have some baseline of health and functionality, this does diminish the plausibility of the assertion that altruism itself contributes to health. Indeed, a nurse–doctor team based at Duke University Medical Center studied health outcomes of patients with coronary artery disease, hypothesizing that volunteerism may improve the health outcomes of patients previously hospitalized with this condition. The authors drew on evidence from the Duke Heart Center Patient Support Program, which is staffed by former cardiac patients who make regular visits to cardiac inpatients at the medical center. The volunteers report that this role provides them with a heightened sense of purpose for continued progress and reduces the despair or depression that is linked to increased mortality in these patients (Sullivan & Sullivan, 1997).

The idea that human beings are inclined toward helpful prosocial and altruistic behavior seems incontrovertible, and it is highly plausible that the inhibition of such behavior and related emotions would be unhealthy. What conceptual models would help explain the connection between altruism and health? Three closely interwoven models can be suggested: evolutionary biology, physiological advantages, and positive emotion.

Evolutionary Psychology

The association between a kind, generous way of life and health prolongevity can be interpreted in the light of evolutionary psychology. Group selection theory, for example, suggests a powerfully adaptive connection between widely diffuse altruism within groups and group survival. Altruistic behavior within groups confers a competitive advantage against other groups that would be selected for (Sober & Wilson, 1998). Members of a successful group would likely be innately oriented to other-regarding behaviors, the inhibition of which would not be salutary. Anthropologists discovered that early egalitarian societies (such as the bushmen) practice institutionalized or "ecological altruism" where helping others is not an act of volunteerism but a social norm. Perhaps those of us in contemporary technological cultures are isolated in various respects and have strayed too far from out altruistic proclivities (Putnam, 2001).

Lee (2003) posits a considerable evolutionary selective pressure for altruistic generativity in older adults. In contrast to other species, human beings live and work well past their reproductive years. Lee suggests intergenerational transfer as an explanatory factor. A species will evolve to the optimal point of investment of older adults in the well-being of grandchildren. In other words, the selective advantage to youth of grandparenting may explain human longevity well past the stage of reproductive potential. There is some evidence that natural selection is at work through the improved survival rates of grandchildren who are helped by both parents and grandparents. This holds true today in a variety of ethnic groups, including the African American community (Gallup & Jones, 1992). A recent study indicates that older veterans with diagnoses of posttraumatic stress disorder (PTSD) show reduced symptoms after caring for their grandchildren (Hierholzer, 2004). If older adults are oriented toward helping behaviors toward grandchildren, this helping inclination can be manifested in a broader social generativity.

Possibilities for Physiologic Advantages

The fight–flight response, with its well-documented physiological cascade, is adaptive in the face of perceived danger. If the threat continues for an extended period, however, the immune and cardiovascular systems are adversely impacted, weakening the body's defense and making it more susceptible to abnormal internal cellular processes involved in malignant degeneration (Sternberg, 2001). Altruistic emotions can gain dominance over anxiety and fear, turning off the fight–flight response. Immediate and unspecified physiological changes may occur as a result of volunteering and helping others, leading to the so-called helper's high (Luks, 1988). Two thirds of helpers report a distinct physical sensation associated with helping; about half report that they experienced a "high" feeling, whereas 43% felt stronger and more energetic, 28% felt warm, 22% felt calmer and less depressed, 21% experienced greater self-worth, and 13% experienced fewer aches and pains. Despite these reports, the physiological changes that occur in the body during the process of helping others have not yet been scientifically studied. However, Field et al. (1998) showed that older adults who volunteer to give massages to infants at a nursery school have lowered stress hormones, including salivary cortisol and plasma norepinephrine and epinephrine. Lowering of cortisol is associated with less stress (Lewis et al., 2000).

These are interesting results that resonate with Reisman's (1965) "helper-therapy principle"—that is, that the agents of helping behavior benefit in many ways. It would be useful to have additional studies of the physiological effects of helping others (Edwards & Cooper, 1988). Students who were simply asked to watch a film about Mother Teresa's work with the poor and sick in Calcutta showed significant increases in the protective antibody salivary immunoglobulin A (S-IgA) when compared with those watching a more neutral film. Moreover, S-IgA remained high for an hour after the film in those participants who were asked to focus their minds on times when they had loved or been loved in the past. Thus, "dwelling on love" strengthened the immune system (McClelland, McClelland, & Kirchnit, 1988; McClelland, 1986).

Positive Emotions May Protect or Distract from Negative Ones

Anderson (2003) of the American Psychological Association highlights six dimensions of health:

- Biology (biological well-being)
- Thoughts and actions (psychological and behavioral well-being)
- Environment and relationships (environmental and social well-being)
- Personal achievement and equality (economic well-being)
- Faith and meaning (existential, religious, spiritual well-being)
- Emotions (emotional well-being)

According to the Anderson (2003) model, positive emotions (kindness, other-regarding love, compassion, etc.) enhance health by virtue of pushing aside negative ones. The generous affect that gives rise to love of humanity is usually associated with a certain delight in the affirmation of others; it seems to cast out the fear and anxiety that emerge from preoccupation with self. Anderson draws on a wealth of studies to conclude that "the big three" negative emotions are "sadness/depression, fear/anxiety, and anger/hostility" (p. 243). It is difficult to be angry, resentful, or fearful when one is showing unselfish love toward another person.

Many emotions can evoke the fight–fight response: stress (fear, anxiety, worry, or sense of time pressure), aggressive emotions (e.g., anger, resentment, or bitterness from unforgiveness), and depressive emotions (e.g., sadness; boredom; loss of purpose, meaning, or hope). The consequences of these negative emotional responses are increased susceptibility to disease and worse health outcomes. Little research has examined the effects of altruistic love (compassion, kindness, desire to help others) on immune or cardiovascular function. Insofar as forgiveness is one manifestation of altruistic love, it has been shown that unforgiving thoughts prompt more aversive emotion and significantly higher heart rate and blood pressure changes from baseline. These finding suggest possible mechanisms through which chronic unforgiving responses (grudges) may erode health, whereas forgiving responses may enhance it (Lawler et al., 2003; Witvliet, Ludwig, & Kelly, 2001).

Of course, further research is always welcome: What more can we learn about altruism as a protective factor against morbidity and mortality in the agent and/or the recipient and about the physiological mediators of the altruism–health relation (e.g., changes in immune function, endorphin production, norepinephrine levels, cortisol levels, and blood pressure)? Does sustained altruism promote health, psychological well-being, and high-level wellness in the agent and/or the recipient over a long time? Under what conditions can altruistic actions become "burdens" rather than sources of meaning and fulfillment, and how do spiritual-religious or other world views come into play? Can new assessment instruments for altruism and altruistic love be developed and validated? How can causality be further clarified?

Public Health Significance and Implications

An altruism–health correlation appears established. Might generous emotions and behaviors be taught as an aspect of mental and physical health in schools and the workplace? Could they even be prescribed by healthcare professionals, as has been discussed ethically with respect to physicians and patient spirituality (Post, Pulchalski, & Larson, 2000)? Can we bring these empirical studies to the training of health care professionals and thereby encourage greater compassionate love in them for their own sake, as well as for therapeutic efficacy?

Research on the benefits of doing good could spark a movement in public health that focuses on civic engagement and helping behavior within communities. So much of public health is rightly focused on environmental toxins and the control of epidemics (McCullough & Snyder, 2000). However, a positive vision of public health must nurture benevolent affect and helping behavior. Rowe and Kahn (1998) point to the public health benefits of volunteerism for older adults. They include a brief discussion of some examples of volunteerism, pointing out that older adults for the most part agree with these two statements: "Life is not worth living if one cannot contribute to the well-being of others" and "Older people who no longer work should contribute through community service" (p. 178). They also point out that "fewer than one-third of all older men and women work as volunteers and those who do spend, on average, fewer than two hours a week on the job" (p. 180). If these figures are correct—and they can be disputed—a firmly established association between helping behavior and longevity might encourage greater volunteerism in older adults. Rowe and Kahn urge voluntary associations to learn how to "reach out to active and able elderly" (p. 180).

The idea of prescribing altruism as a matter of public health is not unprecedented. The notion that there is a connection between a kindly generous life, well-being, happiness, and health has been understood by every mother who has instructed a sullen youngster to "Go out and do something for someone." Current consensus indicates that helping behavior contributes to diminished depression rates in adolescents (Commission on Children at Risk, 2003).

Indeed, the transition in the 1820s in the United States and England from the maltreatment of mentally ill individuals—usually bound in shackles and physically abused—to "moral treatment" was based not only on treating the insane with kindness and sympathy but on occupying their time with chores and other helping behaviors (Clouette & Deslandes, 1997). Another example of the therapeutic use of altruism can be found in the Twelve Steps of Alcoholics Anonymous (AA). Step 12 requires the recovering alcoholic to help other persons with alcoholism. The framework is one of paradox: The recovering individual who helps others with this disease is to do so freely and with no expectation of reward, "And then he discovers that by the divine paradox of this kind of giving he has found his own reward, whether his brother has yet received anything or not" (AA, 1952, p. 109). The AA member finds "no joy greater than in a Twelfth Step job well done" (AA, 1952, p. 110). Those experienced with recovering alcoholics will widely attest as to how important such individuals feel helping others is with regard to their own continued recovery; however, much such helping behavior is in effect an AA recruitment activity. AA is in certain respects a sectarian phenomenon, and such groups do often tap into otherwise inhibited altruistic capacities.

To cite a somewhat more controversial instance of untapped altruism in relation to well-being, Galanter (1999), based on 2 decades of psychiatric research, concluded that young people who join demanding charismatic groups are generally relieved of neurotic distress and depression through enhanced in-group altruism, however much they may be subject to authoritative manipulation and misplaced utopian idealism. It is certainly not always the case that altruistic emotions and behavior are directed in worthwhile ways (Post, 1992).

However, a great deal of altruistic idealism exists outside of such contexts. One of the oldest of the National Opinion Research Center's landmark surveys is the General Social Survey, which has been administered across a national sample of Americans 24 times since 1972. Its 2002 administration, with support from the Fetzer Institute, included an item developed by Dr. Lynn G. Underwood, then with Fetzer, regarding unselfish love: "I feel a selfless caring for others." Based on sample methods of the American population that enjoy the highest level of confidence across a highly diversified sample pool, the following results were found with regard to the previous question: many times a day (9.8% of respondents), every day (13.2% of respondents), most days (20.3% of respondents), some days

(24.0% of respondents), once in a while (22.3% of respondents), and never or almost never (10.4% of respondents). Feelings do not always translate into helping behavior, but these results are cause for hope (Fetzer Institute, 2002).

The essential conclusion of this article is that a strong correlation exists between the well-being, happiness, health, and longevity of people who are emotionally kind and compassionate in their charitable helping activities—as long as they are not overwhelmed, and here world view may come into play. Of course, this is a population generalization that provides no guarantees for the individual. However, there is wisdom in the words of Proverbs 11:25 "a generous man will prosper, he who refreshes others will himself be refreshed" (Revised Standard Version). It can be said that a generous life is a happier and healthier one. The freedom from a solipsistic life in which one relates to others only in so far as they contribute to one's own agendas, as well as a general freedom from the narrow concerns of the self, bring us closer to our true and healthier nature, as all significant spiritual and moral traditions prescribe. Here, epidemiology and the spirituality of love can enter a fruitful dialogue (Levin, 2000). Life can be difficult, and death should not be denied. Love, however, makes the way easier and healthier both for those who give and those who receive.

References

Ainsworth, M., Blehar, M., Waters E., & Wall, S. (1978). *Patterns of attachment: A psychological study of the strange situation.* Mahwah, NJ: Lawrence Erlbaum Associates, Inc.

Alcoholics Anonymous. (1952). *Twelve steps and twelve traditions.* New York: Author.

Anderson, N. B. (2003). *Emotional longevity: What really determines how long you live.* New York: Viking.

Bartrop, R. W., Lazarus, L., Luckhurst, E., Kiloh, L. G., & Penny, R. (1977). Depressed lymphocyte function after bereavement. *Lancet, 1,* 834–836.

Batten, H. L., & Prottas, J. M. (1987). Kind strangers—the families of organ donors. *Health Affairs, 6*(2), 35–47.

Brown, S., Nesse, R. M., Vonokur, A. D., & Smith, D. M. (2003). Providing social support may be more beneficial than receiving it: Results from a prospective study of mortality. *Psychological Science, 14,* 320–327.

Clouette, B., & Deslandes, P. (1997). The Hartford retreat for the insane: An early example of the Use of "moral treatment" in America. *Connecticut Medicine: The Journal of the Connecticut State Medical Society, 61,* 521–527.

Commission on Children at Risk. (2003). *Hardwired to connect: The new scientific case for authoritative communities.* New York: Institute for American Values.

Danner, D. D., Snowdon, D. A., & Friesen, W. V. (2001). Positive emotions in early life and longevity: Findings from the nun study. *Journal of Personality and Social Psychology, 80,* 804–813.

Dulin, P., & Hill, R. (2003). Relationships between altruistic activity and positive and negative affect among low-income older adult service providers. *Aging & Mental Health, 7,* 294–299.

Easterbrook, G. (2003). *The progress paradox: How life gets better while people feel worse.* New York: Random House.

Edwards, J. R., & Cooper, C. L. (1988). "The impacts of positive psychological states on physical health: Review and theoretical framework." *Social Science and Medicine, 27,* 1447–1459.

Epel, S. E., Blackburn, E. S., Lin, J., Dhabhar, F. S., Adler, N. E., Morrow, J. D., & Cawthorn, R. M. (2004). "Accelerated telomere shortening in response to life stress." *Proceedings of the National Academy of Sciences, 101,* 17312–17315.

Fetzer Institute/National Institute on Aging Working Group. (2002). *Multidimensional measurement of religiousness/spirituality for use in health research.* Kalamazoo, MI: The Fetzer Institute.

Field, M. F., Hernandez-Reif, M., Quintino, O., Schanberg, S., & Kuhn C. (1998). Elder retired volunteers benefit from giving message therapy to infants. *Journal of Applied Gerontology, 17,* 229–239.

Frankl, V. E. (1956). *Man's search for meaning.* New York: Pocket Books.

Fredrickson, B. L. (2003). The value of positive emotions: The emerging science of positive psychology is coming to understand why it's good to feel good. *American Scientist, 91,* 330–335.

Galanter, M. (1999). *Cults: Faith, healing, and coercion* (2nd ed.). New York: Oxford University Press.

Gallop, G. H., & Jones, T. (1992). *Saints among us.* New York: Morehouse Group.

Goode, W. J. (1959). The theoretical importance of love. *American Sociological Review, 24,* 38–47.

Goodkin, K., & Visser, A. P. (Eds.). (2000). *Psychoneuroimmunology: Stress, mental disorders and health.* Washington, DC: American Psychiatric Association.

Harlow, H. (1958). The nature of love. *The American Psychologist, 13,* 673–685.

Hendrick, C., & Hendrick, S. (1986). A theory and method of love. *Journal of Personality and Social Psychology, 50,* 392–402.

Hierholzer, R. W. (2004) Improvements in PSTD patients who care for their grandchildren. *American Journal of Psychiatry, 161,* 176.

House, J. S., Robbins, C., & Metzner, H. L. (1982). The association of social relationships and activities with mortality: Prospective evidence from the Tecumseh Community Health Study. *American Journal of Epidemiology, 116,* 123–140.

Hunter, K. I., & Linn, M. W. (1980–1981). Psychosocial differences between elderly volunteers and non-volunteers. *International Journal of Aging and Human Development, 12,* 205–213.

Ironson, G., Solomon, G. F., & Balbin, E. G. (2002). Spirituality and religiousness are associated with long survival, health behaviors, less distress, and lower cortisol in people living with HIV/AIDS. *Annals of Behavioral Medicine, 24,* 34–40.

Isen, A. M. (1987). Positive affect, cognitive processes and social behavior. *Advances in Experimental Social Psychology, 20,* 203–253.

Kiecolt-Glaser, J. K., Preacher, K. J., MacCallum, R. C., Malarkey, W. B., & Glaser, R. (2003). Chronic stress and age-related increases in the proinflammatory cytokine interleukin-6. *Proceedings of the National Academy of Sciences, 100,* 9090–9095.

Krause, N., Ingersoll-Dayton, B., Liang, J., & Sugisawa, H. (1999). Religion, social support, and health among the Japanese elderly. *Journal of Health & Social Behavior, 40,* 405–421.

Krueger, R. F., Hicks, B. M., & McGue, M. (2001). Altruism and antisocial behavior: Independent tendencies, unique personality correlates, distinct etiologies. *Psychological Science, 12,* 397–402.

Lee, R. D. (2003). Rethinking the evolutionary theory of aging: Transfers, not births, shape senescence in social species. *Proceedings of the National Academy of Sciences, 100,* 9637–9642.

Levin, J. (2000). A prolegomenon to an epidemiology of love: Theory, measurement, and health outcomes. *Journal of Social and Clinical Psychology, 19,* 117–136.

Lewis, T., Amini, F., & Lannon, R. (2000). *A general theory of love.* New York: Random House.

Liang, J., Krause, N. M., & Bennett, J. M. (2001). Social exchange and well-being: Is giving better than receiving? *Psychology & Aging, 16,* 511–523.

Lawler, K. A., Youner, J. W., Piferi, R. L., Billington, E., Jobe, R., Edmundson, K., & Jones, W. H. (2003). A change of heart: Cardiovascular correlates of forgiveness in response to interpersonal conflict. *Journal of Behavioral Medicine, 26,* 373–393.

Luks, A. (1988, October). Helper's high: Volunteering makes people feel good, physically and emotionally. And like "runner's calm," it's probably good for your health. *Psychology Today, 22*(10), 34–42.

McClelland, D. C. (1986). Some reflections on the two psychologies of love. *Journal of Personality, 54,* 334–353.

McClelland, D., McClelland, D. C., & Kirchnit, C. (1988). The effect of motivational arousal through films on salivary immunoglobulin A. *Psychology and Health, 2,* 31–52.

McCullough, M. E., & Snyder, C. R. (2000). Classical sources of human strength: Revisiting an old home and building a new one. *Journal of Social and Clinical Psychology, 19,* 1–10.

Medalie, J. H., & Goldbourt, U. (1976). Angina pectoris among 10,000 men. II. Psychosocial and other risk factors as evidenced by a multivariate analysis of a five year incidence study. *American Journal of Medicine, 60,* 910–921.

Medalie, J. H., Stange, K. C., Zyzanski, S. J., & Goldbourt, U. (1992). The importance of biopsychosocial factors in the development of duodenal ulcer in a cohort of middle-aged men. *American Journal of Epidemiology, 136,* 1280–1287.

Midlarsky, E. (1991). Helping as coping. *Prosocial Behavior: Review of Personality and Social Psychology, 12,* 238–264.

Midlarsky, E., & Kahana, E. (1994). *Altruism in later life.* Thousand Oaks, CA: Sage.

Moen, P., Dempster-McCain, D., & Williams, R. M. (1993). Successful aging. *American Journal of Sociology, 97,* 1612–1632.

Morrow-Howell, N., Hinterlonh, J., Rozario, P. A., & Tang, F. (2003). Effects of volunteering on the well-being of older adults. *Journals of Gerontology Series B-Psychological Sciences Social Sciences, 58*(3), S137–145.

Musick, M. A., Herzog, A. R., & House, J. S. (1999). Volunteering and mortality among older adults: Findings from a national sample. *Journals of Gerontology Series B-Psychological Sciences Social Sciences, 54*(3), S173–S180.

Musick, M. A., & Wilson, J. (2003). Volunteering and depression: The role of psychological and social resources in different age groups. *Social Science & Medicine, 56,* 259–269.

Nerem, R. M., Levesque, M. J., & Cornhill, J. F. (1980). Social environment as a factor in diet-induced atherosclerosis. *Science, 208,* 1475–1476.

Oman, D., & Reed, D. (1998). Religion and mortality among community-dwelling elderly. *American Journal of Public Health, 88,* 1469–1475.

Oman, D., Thoresen, C. E., & McMahon, K. (1999). Volunteerism and mortality among the community-dwelling elderly. *Journal of Health Psychology, 4,* 301–316

Omoto, A., & Snyder, M. (1995). Sustained helping without obligation: Motivation, longevity of service, and perceived attitude change among AIDS volunteers. *Journal of Personality and Social Psychology, 16,* 152–166.

Ornish, D. (1999). *Love and survival: The scientific basis for the healing power of intimacy.* New York: Perennial Currents.

Post, S. G. (1992). DSM-III-R and religion. *Social Science and Medicine, 35,* 81–90.

Post, S. G. (2002). *Unlimited love—altruism, compassion, service.* Philadelphia: Templeton Foundation Press.

Post, S. G. (Ed.). (2004). *The encyclopedia of bioethics* (3rd ed.). New York: Macmillan Reference.

Post, S. G., & Binstock, R. H. (Eds.). (2004). *The fountain of youth: Cultural, scientific and ethical perspectives on a biomedical goal.* New York: Oxford University Press.

Post, S. G., Pulchalski, C. M., & Larson, D. B. (2000). Physicians and patient spirituality: Professional boundaries, competency, and ethics. *Annals of Internal Medicine, 132,* 578–583.

Post, S. G., Underwood, L. G., Schloss, J. R., & Hurlbut, W. B. (2002). *Altruism and altruistic love: Science, philosophy and religion in dialogue.* New York: Oxford University Press.

Putnam, R. D. (2001). *Bowling alone: The collapse and revival of American culture.* New York: Simon & Schuster.

Rees, W. D., & Lutkins, S. G. (1967). Mortality of bereavement. *British Medical Journal, 4,* 13–16.

Reisman, F. (1965). The 'helper' therapy principle. *Social Work, 10,* 27–37.

Russek, L. G., & Schwartz, G. E. (1997). Perceptions of parental caring predict health status in midlife: A 35-year follow-up of the Harvard Mastery of Stress Study. *Psychosomatic Medicine, 59,* 144–149.

Rotzien, A., Vacha-Haase, T., Murthy, K., Davenport, D., & Thompson, B. A. (1994). A confirmatory factor analysis of the Hendrick-Hendrick love attitudes scale: We may not yet have an acceptable model. *Structural Equation Modeling, 1,* 360–374.

Rowe, J. W., & Kahn, R. L. (1998). *Successful aging.* New York: Pantheon.

Russek, L. G., & Schwartz, G. E. (1997). Feelings of parental caring predict health status in midlife: A 35 year follow-up of the Harvard Mastery of Stress Study. *Journal of Behavioral Medicine, 20,* 1–13.

Sapolsky, R. M. (2004). Organismal stress and telomeric aging: An unexpected connection. *Proceedings of the National Academy of Sciences, 101,* 17323–17324.

Schwartz, C., Meisenhelder, J. B., Ma, Y., & Reed, G. (2003). Altruistic social interest behaviors are associated with better mental health. *Psychosomatic Medicine, 65,* 778–785.

Sober, E., & Wilson, D. S. (1998). *Unto others: The evolution of unselfish behavior.* Cambridge, MA: Harvard University Press.

Sorokin, P. A. (2002). *The ways and power of love: Types, factors, and techniques of moral transformation.* Philadelphia: Templeton Press. (original work published in 1954)

Sternberg, E. M. (2001). *The balance within: The science connecting health and emotions.* New York: Freeman.

Sternberg, R. J., & Barnes, M. L. (Eds.). (1988). *The psychology of love.* New Haven, CT: Yale University Press.

Sullivan, G. B., & Sullivan, M. J. (1997). Promoting wellness in cardiac rehabilitation: Exploring the role of altruism. *Journal of Cardiovascular Nursing, 11*(3), 43–52.

Vaillant, G. E. (2002). *Aging well.* Boston: Little, Brown.

Witvliet, C. V., Ludwig, T. E., & Kelly, L. V. L. (2001). Granting forgiveness or harboring grudges: Implications for emotion, physiology and health. *Psychological Science, 12,* 117–123.

Young, F. W., & Glasgow, N. (1998). Voluntary social participation & health. *Research on Aging, 20,* 339–362.

Zisook, S., ed. (1987). *Biopsychosocial aspects of bereavement.* Cambridge, UK: Cambridge University Press.

Representative List of Cited Research and Major Findings

Reference/ Author	Study Focus	Key Findings
Danner et al., 2001	Nuns short stories and Alzheimers disease	Nuns who expressed the most positive emotions lived 10 years longer and were also somewhat protected from dementia
Fredrickson, 2003	Summary article	When people feel good, their thinking becomes more creative, integrative, flexible, and open to information
		Positive emotions enhanced psychological and physical resistance
Health benefits for recipients (those who receive compassionate love)		
Nerem et al., 1980	Affectionate care of rabbits (petting, etc.)	60% less arthrosclerosis
Medalie and Goldbourt, 1976	Loving and supported wives (perception of)	Half the rate of angina for husbands who perceived their wives as being loving and supportive vs. those who felt unloved and unsupported
Medalie et al., 1992	A wife's love	Lowered risk of duodenal ulcers
Russek and Schwartz, 1997	Perceptions of love felt from parents	91% who did not perceive that they had warm relationships with their mothers had midlife diseases (coronary artery disease, high blood pressure, duodenal ulcer, and alcoholism) vs. 45% who reported having a warm relationship with their mothers
		82% of low warmth and closeness with their father has such diagnosis vs. 50% who reported high warmth and closeness
		100% who reported low warmth and closeness from both parents had midlife diagnoses of diseases
Epel et al., 2004	Stress accelerates aging	Women with highest levels of perceived stress had telomeres that were, on average, shortened by one decade vs. low stress women
Altruism, happiness and health		
Huner and Linn, 1981	Retires older than 65 who volunteered	Volunteers significantly higher on life satisfaction and will to live and fewer symptoms of depression, anxiety, and somatization
Dulin and Hill, 2003; Liang et al., 2001: Morrow-Howell, et al., 2003	Studies of older adults	Association between altruistic activities and well-being and life satisfaction
Midlarsky and Kahana, 1994	Adult altruism associated with well-being, happiness	Improved morale, self-esteem, positive affect, and well being
Volunteerism		
Musick and Wilson, 2003	Volunteerism	Reduction in depressive symptoms
Krueger et al., 2001	Volunteerism	Happiness, enhanced well-being
Schwartz et al., 2003	Altruistic social behaviors effect on mental and physical health (anxiety and depression)	Giving help was more significantly associated with better mental health than was receiving help. But "feeling overwhelmed by others' demands has a stronger negative relationship with mental health than helping others had a positive one."
Moen et al., 1993	Physical health of mothers who volunteered over a 30-year period	52% who did not belong to a volunteer organization had experienced a major illness vs. only 36% for those who did belong to one
Musik et al., 1999	Volunteerism and risk of death	Moderate amount of volunteerism associated with lower risk of death
Oman, Thoressen, and McMahon, 1999	Volunteerism and risk of death	Those who volunteered for 2 or more organizations had a 63% lower likelihood of dying during the study period than non-volunteers.
		After controlling for health status:
		44% reduction in mortality associated with high volunteerism
		39% reduction with physical mobility
		30% reduction for exercising 4 times a week
		29% reduction for weekly religious service attendance.
		49% reduction for not smoking

Reference/ Author	Study Focus	Key Findings
Krause et al., 1999	Study of older adults in Japan	Those who provided more assistance to others were significantly more likely to indicate that their physical health was better
Ironson et al., 2002	Study of Long Term AIDS survivors	Survivors were significantly more likely to be spiritual or religious
		This effect was mediated by "helping others with HIV"
Brown et al., 2003	Older couples	Found an association between reduced risk of dying and giving help, but no association between receiving help and reduced death risk
		"Those who provided no instrumental or emotional support to others were more than twice as likely to die in the five years as people who helped (others)"
	Miscellaneous other studies cited	
Sullivan and Sullivan, 1997	Duke study of post coronary artery disease volunteers (after their heart attacks)	Volunteers reported a heightened sense of purpose and reduced sense of despair or depression that is linked to increased mortality in these patients
Hierholzer, 2004	Older veterans with posttraumatic stress disorder (PTSD)	Showed reduced symptoms after caring for their grandchildren
Luks, 1988	"Helper's high"	Two thirds of helpers report a distinct physical sensation associated with helping:
		About half report a "high" feeling
		43% felt stronger and more energetic
		28% felt warm
		22% felt calmer and less depressed
		21% felt greater self-worth
		13% experienced fewer aches and pains
Field et al., 1998	Older adults massaging infants	Lowered stress hormones, including salivary cortisol and plasma norepinephrine and epinephrine
McClelland et al., 1988	Watching a film about Mother Teresa's work, or "dwelling on love"	Significant increase in the protective salivary immunoglobin A (S-IgA)
Commission on Children at Risk, 2003	Adolescents and depression	Helping behavior contributes to diminished depression rates in adolescents (current consensus)

International Journal of Behavioral Medicine
2005, Vol. 12, No. 2, 78–85

Life Meaning: An Important Correlate of Health in the Hungarian Population

Árpád Skrabski, Maria Kopp, Sándor Rózsa, János Réthelyi, and Richard H. Rahe

One of the 5 coping scales in Rahe's Brief Stress and Coping Inventory, entitled Life Meaning, was examined in relation to demographic characteristics, other coping measures, and health status in a sample of 12,640 Hungarian participants. Participants were selected to represent the country's population according to sex, age, and place of residence. The study also explored the contribution of life meaning to the explanation of variations of middle-aged (45–64 years) male and female mortality rates across 150 subregions in Hungary. On an ecological level life meaning proved to be inversely related to male and female oncological, female cardiovascular, and total premature mortality rates in the 150 subregions of Hungary and on an individual level to participants' reported health status. In the total sample of individuals after controlling for gender, age, and education, life meaning scores showed strong correlations with the World Health Organization well-being scale, with self-rated absence of depression, with self-rated health, and with self-rated absence of disability. Although relatively unrelated to age, gender, and education, life meaning was positively related to self-efficacy, importance of religion, problem-oriented coping, and social support.

Key words: life meaning, premature oncological mortality, premature cardiovascular mortality, self-rated health, well-being, depression, self-efficacy, spirituality, religion, ways of coping, social support

In modern-day Central-Eastern European countries, there is a morbidity and mortality crisis, involving chiefly the middle-aged population. (Cornia & Panicia, 2001). Up through the end of the 1970s, mortality rates in Hungary were lower than those observed in Great Britain or Austria. Subsequently, mortality rates de-clined in Western Europe. However, in Hungary and in other Central-Eastern European countries this trend was reversed, especially among middle-aged men. In the late 1980s, the mortality rates among 45- to 64-year-old men in Hungary rose to and remained at levels that were higher than they were in the 1930s (Demographic Yearbook, 2002; Kopp & Réthelyi, 2004; Kopp, Skrabski, & Szedmák, 2000; Skrabski, Kopp, & Kawachi, 2003, 2004). Between 1970 and 1990, mortality rates increased from 12.5 to 15.5 per thousand for men and from 10.8 to 12.8 per thousand for women (Demographic Yearbook, 2002; Kopp, Skrabski, & Székely, 2002). In Hungarian persons younger than 65 years, the standardized mortality rates for cardiovascular disorders are three times higher and for oncological disorders twice as high as the European average. In Hungary, deaths due to neoplasms are among the highest in international comparisons (Gárdos, 2002).

The most popular explanations for health trends in Central-Eastern Europe do not provide an explanation for these sudden changes in health status (Cornia & Paniccia, 2001; Piko, 2004). Thus, there is a need for new approaches to understanding the processes of health deterioration in societies in transition. In a recent review, Pikó and Fitzpatrick (2004) suggested that understanding and solving the Central-Eastern European health crisis required creative psychological approaches.

Árpád Skrabski, Vilmos Apor Catholic College, Vác, Hungary; Maria Kopp, János Réthelyi, Institute of Behavioural Sciences, Semmelweis University, Budapest, Hungary; Sándor Rózsa, Institute of Psychology, Eötvös Loránt University, Budapest, Hungary; Richard H. Rahe, Veterans Affairs Puget Sound Health Care System, American Lake Division, Tacoma, WA, USA

The authors would like to thank Professor Gail Ironson and Professor Lynda Powell for their valuable advice and suggestions for the improvement of the manuscript; the other members of the "Hungarostudy 2002" team (Adrienne Stauder, Csilla Csoboth, Éva Susánszky, György Gyukits, János Lőke, Andrea Ódor, András Székely, and László Szűcs); the network of district nurses for the home interviews; Professor András Klinger for the sampling procedure; and especially to Katalin Hajdu, Csilla Raduch, and Noémi Somorjai for valuable assistance in the study. This study was supported by the United Nations Development Program (UNDP) project No. HUN/00/002/A/01/99, the National Research Fund (OTKA) projects No. T–32974 (2000), OTKA TS–40889 (2002), and T (2004) Scientific School grant, NKFP 1/002/2001 and NKFP 1b/020/2004.

Correspondence concerning this article should be addressed to Professor Maria Kopp, Institute of Behavioural Sciences, Semmelweis University Budapest, H–1089 Budapest, Nagyvárad tér 4, Hungary. E-mail: kopmar@net.sote.hu

Premature mortality is the most dramatic measure of poor health in a society. However, a broader concept of health is to view it as a dynamic equilibrium. The World Health Organization (WHO) definition of health emphasizes the importance of mental and social well-being (WHO, 2001). This concept, by definition, draws on the contributions of positive psychology, which aim to understand and reinforce human strengths and factors that allow individuals, communities, and societies to flourish (Seligman & Csikszentmihályi, 2000).

Empirical evidence suggests beneficial health effects from individuals' spiritual beliefs and practices. Spirituality appears to be an important resource for health and one that is not easily reducible to other social and behavioral factors such as social support and socioeconomic status (for reviews see Astrow, Puchalsky, & Sulmasy, 2001; Miller & Thoresen, 2003; Oman & Thoresen, 2003; Powell, Shahabi, & Thoresen, 2003). Spirituality is a broader concept than religion, not limited to those who practice some religious tradition, and is frequently about a search for transcendent meaning (Astrow et al., 2001; Powell et al., 2003).

The Life Meaning subscale of Rahe's Brief Stress and Coping Inventory examines one component of spirituality (Appendix). Some questions are similar to the meaningfulness component of Antonovsky's (1993) Sense of Coherence questionnaire. However, it also includes questions related to the transcendent meaning of life, such as "I feel my life is part of a larger plan" and "My values and beliefs guide me daily."

There were two aims of this study. First, we aimed to determine the relation between Rahe's life meaning construct and self-reported health in a large, representative sample of the Hungarian population. Second, we aimed to determine the ecologic variation between life meaning scores and rates of total, cardiovascular, and oncological morality in middle-aged men and women living in 150 subregions in Hungary.

Methodology

Sample

The Hungarostudy 2002 is a national, cross-sectional survey that is representative of the Hungarian population older than 18 years according to sex, age, and the 150 subregions in the country. The sampling was carried out using the National Population Register, which was updated using the 2001 National Census. A clustered, stratified sampling procedure was developed by experts at the National Population Register. All communities with a population of more than 10,000 were included in the sample as well as a randomly selected sample of smaller villages. In a second step, single persons were selected from this database in an age and gender distribution that was comparable to that existing in the specific county or settlement size from which they were drawn. The final sample thus reflected the gender, age, and settlement size characteristics of each given county. Two random samples of 13,000 persons were generated. The first sample was used for the study, and the second sample allowed for replacements of individuals in the first sample who refused to participate.

In 2002, 12,643 persons were interviewed in their homes (Rózsa et al., 2003; Skrabski et al., 2004). The sample represented 0.16% of the population older than age 18. The refusal rate was 17.7%. There were differences in refusals based on residence where refusals tended to be higher in large cities than in small villages and based on gender where refusals were 4% higher in men than in women. For each refusal, another person was selected of the same age and sex from the same community. This replacement procedure did not result in any significant selection bias. The final sample corresponded well to the population descriptors of the Central Statistical Office. We compared the distributions of selected important variables in the final dataset and in the original. The sampling error in each case was within statistically acceptable limits with the highest estimated stratification error being 2.2% in men aged 18–39. This error is within the limits of the permitted statistical deviation (Rózsa et al., 2003).

The interviewers in this study were district nurses, and the time spent in the homes administrating the questionnaires was approximately 1 hr each (Skrabski et al., 2004). Because of their education in health, district nurses were selected as the most competent persons for interviewing our participants. These nurses were intensively trained for their duties over a 2-week period, including personal supervision and three test interviews before they began data collection.

Standardized Mortality Data

Ecological mortality analyses drew on age-standardized, midlife (45–64 years), gender-specific mortality rates for the main causes of death computed by the Central Statistical Office of Hungary for each of the 150 Hungarian subregions for the last available years, between 2001 and 2003 (Klinger, 2004). The standardized, weighted cardiovascular (International Classification of Diseases (ICD) 10, 100–199), oncological (ICD 10, C00–D48), and total mortality rates were included as outcome measures.

Measures

Life meaning. The Hungarian translation of this eight-item subscale from the Brief Stress and Coping Inventory of Richard Rahe (Rahe et al, 2002; Rahe & Tolles, 2002; Rahe, Veach, Tolles, & Murakami, 2000) was included in the analyses (See Appendix). Cronbach's α for this scale was 0.69 in this study, indicative of acceptable internal consistency (Rózsa et al., 2003). The life meaning score was normally distributed in the sample (0 = lowest score, 16 = maximal score).

Depression. Depressive symptomatology was measured by the nine-item shortened version of the Beck Depression Inventory (BDI). This is a reliable measure for screening depressive symptom severity in community surveys (Kopp & Skrabski, 1996; Kopp et al., 2000; Lasa, Ayuso-Mateos, Vazquez-Barquero, Diez-Manrique, & Dowrick, 2000; Rózsa, Szádóczky, & Füredi, 2001). In this study the internal consistency for this scale was 0.85 (Rózsa et al., 2003). The Hungarian version of this scale was validated in the general population and on clinical samples earlier (Rózsa et al., 2001; 0 = lowest score, 27 = maximal score).

WHO Well-Being Scale. This five-item measure of well-being had a Cronbach's α of 0.84 in this study (Bech, Staehr-Johansen, & Gudex, 1996; Rózsa et al., 2003; 0 = lowest score, 15 = maximal score).

Self-Efficacy questionnaire. Cronbach's α for this four-item scale in this study was 0.83 (Kopp, Schwarzer, & Jerusalem, 1993; Rózsa et al., 2003; Schwarzer, 1993; 0 = lowest score, 12 = maximal score).

Shortened version of Ways of Coping questionnaire. The 16-item shortened version of the Ways of Coping questionnaire (Folkman & Lazarus, 1980; Kopp & Skrabski, 1996; Rózsa et al., 2003) features problem-focused coping (0 = lowest score, 18 = maximal score), emotion-focused coping (0 = lowest score, 24 = maximal score), and support seeking (0 = lowest score, 6 = maximal score) factors (Rózsa et al., in press; Skrabski et al., 2004). Cronbach's α for the total score was 0.71 in this study (Rózsa et al., 2003).

Perceived social support. This scale measured perceived support separately as support from family members (0 = no support, 15 = maximal support); from nonfamily members (0 = no support, 12 = maximal support); and from civic associations, religious associations, or both (0 = no support, 6 = maximal support; Caldwell et al., 1987; Kopp & Skrabski, 1996; Kopp et al., 2000). Each type of support was scored from 0 to 3, indicating the degree of perceived support ranging from none to a great deal.

Subjectively rated health (SRH) and self-reported disability (SRD). SRH was measured with the question "How do you rate your health in general?" There were five responses: very good, good, fair, poor, and very poor. Self-reported absence of SRD was mea-

sured by the question "How do you rate your working disability?" There were six response options: no working disability, light working disability, medium working disability, severe working disability, not able to work, and cannot leave his or her chair or bedridden.

Religious involvement and importance of religion. Involvement in religion was measured by two questions: "Are you religious? If yes, what is the form of your worship?" Responses to the first question were scored 0 for "I am not religious," 1 for "I don't worship," 2 for "I worship in my own way," 3 for "I worship rarely in my church," and 4 for "I worship regularly in my church." The second question related to the importance of religion was scored 0 for "Not at all," 1 for "Slightly," 2 for "Very important," and 3 for "It influences my every action."

Demographic control variables. Education was measured by the highest education grade on a six-level score (from less than primary to university level). Sex (1 = men, 2 = women) and age of the persons were included.

Statistical Methods

SPSS (1999a,b) Base 9 was used for all analyses. Cronbach α coefficients, partial correlation analyses, and multiple stepwise linear regression analyses with standardized β weights were used. Partial correlation coefficients, adjusting for age, sex, and education, were calculated between life meaning and self-rated health, self-rated freedom from disability, and the other psychosocial variables on an individual level. Regression models were constructed to examine life meaning jointly with the other demographic and psychosocial variables as correlates of the various self-reported health dependent variables. For the ecological analyses, the average values of life meaning scores were computed for each of the 150 Hungarian subregions, separately for men and women, and then correlated with gender- and disease-specific mortality rates for each of these subregions.

Results

Table 1 presents the results of the ecological analyses that link average life meaning scores to standardized subregional mortality rates in each of the 150 subregions in Hungary (weighted by number of cases; men and women in 45–64 year age group; $n = 4,265$, female $= 2,274$, male $= 1,991$). Life meaning was inversely related to premature total and oncological mortality for both men and women. For cardiovascular mortality, life meaning was inversely related only for the women. Male total premature mortality and male cardiovascu-

Table 1. *Ecological Correlations Between Standardized Oncological, Cardiovascular, and Total Mortality Rates and Average Life Meaning Scores in 150 Hungarian Subregions, in 45–64 Year-Old Men and Women*

	Average Male Life Meaning		Average Female Life Meaning	
Male oncological mortality	$r = -.190$,	$p < 0.000$	$r = -.185$,	$p < 0.000$
Male cardiovascular mortality	$r = -.011$,	ns	$r = -.056$,	$p < 0.000$
Male total mortality	$r = -.089$,	$p < 0.000$	$r = -.108$,	$p < 0.000$
Female oncological mortality	$r = -.043$,	$p < 0.005$	$r = -.032$,	$p < 0.038$
Female cardiovascular mortality	$r = -.039$,	$p < 0.010$	$r = -.110$,	$p < 0.000$
Female total mortality	$r = -.029$,	ns	$r = -.062$,	$p < 0.000$

Note. Weighted by number cases, men and women in 45–64 years age group. $n = 4,265$, male 1,991, female 2,274. ns= not significant.

lar mortality were more closely connected with female life meaning than with male life meaning.

Table 2 presents the results of the individual level analyses linking life meaning to self-reported health. After controlling for the effects of gender, age and education, life meaning was most closely connected with

Table 2. *Partial Correlations Between Life Meaning and Self-Reported Health*

	Life Meaning Score	
WHO well-being	$r = .349^a$	$p < 0.000$
Self-rated absence of depression	$r = .261^a$	$p < 0.000$
Self rated health	$r = .172^a$	$p < 0.000$
Self-rated freedom from disability	$r = .118^a$	$p < 0.000$

Note. $n = 12,640$. WHO = World Health Organization.
[a]Controlled for sex, age, and education.

WHO well-being score ($r = .349$), next with the self-rated absence of depression ($r = .261$), with self-rated health ($r = .172$), and with self-rated absence of disability ($r = .118$). All correlations were highly significant ($p < 0.000$).

Tables 3–5 present the results of the regression analyses that examine the independent correlates of well-being, depression, and self-rated health, respectively. Table 3 shows that the most important correlate of WHO well-being was life meaning where the β weight (.27) was more than twice that of the next strongest variable (age) to enter the equation. Table 4 shows that the three most important correlates of BDI depression were life meaning ($\beta = -.20$), age ($\beta = .22$), and emotion-focused coping ($\beta = .26$). Table 5 shows that the most important correlate of self-rated health was age ($\beta = -.42$). After age and education, life meaning entered third in the model ($\beta = .11$).

Table 3. *Independent Correlates of WHO Well-Being Score*

Stepwise Linear Regression	Standardized βs	t	Sig.	Adjusted R Squared for the Final Model
Life meaning	.27	24.99	< 0.000	12
Age	−.14	−13.56	< 0.000	16
Problem-focused coping	.12	11.32	< 0.000	17
Emotion-focused coping	−.11	−11.43	< 0.000	18
Perceived help, not from relatives	.07	6.76	0.000	19
Sex	−.08	−8.35	< 0.000	19
Education	.06	6.48	< 0.000	20
Perceived help from family	.03	3.12	< 0.001	20

Notes. $n = 12,640$. WHO = World Health Organization.

Table 4. *Independent Correlates of Shortened Beck Depression Score*

Stepwise Linear Regression	Standardized βs	t	Sig.	Adjusted R Squared for the Final Model
Life meaning	−.20	−18.81	< 0.000	.07
Age	.22	22.03	< 0.000	.13
Emotion-focused coping	.26	26.19	< 0.000	.20
Education	−.16	−16.30	< 0.000	.23
Perceived help, not from relatives	−.06	−6.59	< 0.000	.23
Sex	.05	5.26	< 0.000	.24
Perceived help from civic or religious association	.04	4.59	< 0.000	.24
Perceived help from family	−.04	−4.12	< 0.000	.24
Problem-focused coping	−.03	−2.96	< 0.001	.24

Note. $n = 12,640$.

Table 5. *Independent Correlates of Self-Rated Health*

Stepwise Linear Regression	Standardized βs	t	Sig.	Adjusted R Squared for the Final Model
Age	−.42	−43.27	< 0.000	.21
Education	.15	16.37	< 0.000	.25
Life meaning	.11	10.84	< 0.000	.27
Emotion-focused coping	−.11	−12.37	< 0.000	.28
Perceived help, not from relatives	.06	6.14	< 0.000	.29
Problem-focused coping	.04	4.46	< 0.000	.29
Sex	−.03	−3.85	< 0.000	.29

Note. n = 12,640.

Table 6 presents the partial correlations between life meaning and the other psychosocial variables, adjusting for sex, age, and education. Life meaning was most strongly related to self-efficacy (r = .438), but all of the other psychosocial variables were also significantly correlated. There was a connection between life meaning and both practice of religion (r = .187) and importance of religion (r = .221).

Table 7 presents a multivariate model that examines the independent correlates of life meaning. Self-efficacy, importance of religion, problem-focused coping,

Table 6. *Partial Correlations Between Life Meaning and Other Psychosocial Variables*

	Life Meaning Score	
Self-efficacy	r = .438[a]	p < 0.000
Problem-focused coping	r = .339[a]	p < 0.000
Emotion-focused coping	r = −.091[a]	p < 0.000
Perceived social support from relatives	r = .169[a]	p < 0.000
Perceived social support, not from relatives (friends, coworkers, neighbors)	r = .221[a]	p < 0.000
Perceived social support from civic organizations	r = .191[a]	p < 0.000
Importance of religion	r = .221[a]	p < 0.000
Practice of religion	r = .187[a]	p < 0.000

Note. n = 12,640.
[a]Controlled for sex, age, and education.

and perceived social support from nonrelative and from family were most closely connected with life meaning. Sex, age, and education were less closely related. Together, the set of variables explained 33.6% of the variance of life meaning in the total population.

Discussion

Life meaning, as measured by the Rahe Brief Stress and Coping Inventory, proved to be strongly related to the self-reported health status of this large, nationally representative sample of the Hungarian population. On an ecological level, life meaning was also related to premature mortality trends in the 150 subregions of Hungary. Interestingly, male premature mortality and male cardiovascular mortality were more closely connected to female life meaning scores than to male life meaning scores. These results are consistent with our previous findings that male and female health are strongly interconnected but that female attitudes appear to influence male health more strongly than the male attitudes influence female health (Kopp et al., 2004b; Skrabski et al., 2003).

Self-rated health is a reliable predictor of morbidity and mortality. Several studies have shown an increased risk of death in those who report that their health is poor (Idler & Benyamini,1997; Kaplan et al., 1996; Miilunpalo, Vuori, Oja, Pasanen, & Urponen, 1997;

Table 7. *Independent Correlates of Life Meaning*

Stepwise Linear Regression	Standardized βs	t	Sig.	Adjusted R Squared for the Final Model
Self-efficacy	.337	34.7	< 0.000	.198
Importance of religion	.172	16.7	< 0.000	.248
Problem-focused coping	.226	22.3	< 0.000	.292
Social support not from relatives	.104	10.5	< 0.000	.307
Emotion-focused coping	−.105	−11.1	< 0.000	.320
Social support from family	.093	10.1	< 0.000	.329
Social support from religious or civic groups	.057	5.7	< 0.000	.331
Sex	.043	4.7	< 0.000	.333
Age	.049	4.9	< 0.000	.334
Education	.045	4.7	< 0.001	.336

Note. n = 12,640.

Moller, Kristenson, & Hollnagel, 1996; Wannamethee & Shaper, 1991). In a separate study, we examined the ecological associations between self-rated health and middle-aged (45–64 years) mortality rates across the 20 counties of Hungary. We found that self-rated health at the aggregate level is strongly correlated with mortality rates in both men and women, although more strongly for the former than for the latter (Kopp et al., 2004b).

Depression is an independent risk factor for mortality, especially among men (Hemingway & Marmot, 1999; Kubzansky & Kawachi, 2000; Musselman, Evans, & Nemeroff, 1998). Glassman and Shapiro (1998) reviewed the relation between depression and cardiovascular morbidity and mortality. After controlling for smoking and other standard risk factors (gender, weight, activity, blood pressure, and cholesterol), the apparently healthy individuals who had elevated depression ratings were more likely both to develop and to die from ischemic heart disease. The results of five longitudinal studies showed that people with serious depression, and with no cardiovascular disease at the beginning of the study, were two to four times more likely to die of myocardial infarction. This relation held when these data were standardized for other known risk factors (Glassman & Shapiro, 1998; Murphy, Monson, Olivier, Sobol, & Leighton, 1987; Musselman et al., 1998; Pratt et al., 1996). Depression can make the course of other disorders, such as cancer, diabetes, immunological diseases, and osteoporosis, more serious and accelerate aging (Dinan, 1999; Horrobin & Bennett, 1999; Kielkolt-Glaser et al., 2002).

Consequently, our results suggest that meaning in life is an important salutogenic factor in population health, particularly in a society undergoing considerable political and economic transition. The self-efficacy concept (Bandura, 1997; Schwarzer, 1993) is a well-documented positive psychology component, but life meaning was more closely connected to reported good health in our study. Life meaning was, in fact, correlated with a number of positive psychosocial factors, including self-efficacy, problem-focused coping, religiousness, and high levels of social support. Interestingly, life meaning was relatively independent of age, gender, and education.

There is a scholarly neglect of the empowering functions of spirituality in the Western world (Oman & Thoresen, 2003). There are few studies on the health effects of the oppression against spirituality and religion in the communist countries under the Soviet rule. Religion was regarded as "the opium of the people" and Marxist "scientific materialism" was a requirement for university entrance examinations as well as for positions in education, science, and public affairs. Religious practices and expression of spiritual thinking were punished. It can be hypothesized that there were ill-health effects secondary to this strong opposition of religion and spirituality. These proposed effects might be called "cultural iatrogenesis," which diminished the capacities of people to cope positively with difficulties of life (Oman & Thoresen, 2003).

Recent political changes and the uncritical acceptance of Western consumer values in the Hungarian population might also contribute to the health deterioration of the male population. Interestingly, in the older age groups (older than 65 years), the Hungarian health statistics are relatively better than they are in the middle-aged population. Nonetheless, the Hungarian statistics are comparable to the worst Western European figures in the elderly age groups (Demographic Yearbook, 2002; Kopp et al., 2002). The Hungarian health deterioration has been more marked among men than among women in the last decade. Both life meaning and religiousness are higher in women (Kopp et al., 2004c). Religious involvement may be a strong protective factor for the female Hungarian population (Skrabski et al., 2004). It is important to stress, however, that religion and life meaning are not identical concepts. There are religious people with relatively low life meaning and nonreligious people with high life meaning. Thus, life meaning seems to be an independent positive psychological health protective factor, yet one that is closely connected with spirituality and the search for transcendent meaning in life (Astrow et al., 2001).

Meaning in life appears to be a positive psychological resource that promotes health in the Hungarian population. It is possible that a similar finding would emerge from studies of other transitioning societies in Central-Eastern Europe. We encourage the incorporation of life meaning into other large-scale studies of stress, coping, and health in such countries in transition.

APPENDIX
Life Meaning From Rahe's Brief Stress and Coping Inventory

Answers: 0 = no, 1 = sometimes, 2 = frequently

I feel my life is part of a larger plan
My life has no direction and meaning
 (reverse coded)
Many things in life give me great joy
I am able to forgive myself and others
I doubt that my life makes a difference
 (reverse coded)
My values and beliefs guide me daily
I feel in tune with people around me
I am at peace with my place in life

(Rahe & Tolles, 2002; Rahe et al., 2000.)

References

Antonovsky, A. (1993). The structure and properties of the Sense of Coherence Scale. *Social Science & Medicine, 36,* 725–733.

Astrow, A. B., Puchalsky, Ch. M., & Sulmasy, D. P. (2001). Religion, spirituality, and health care: Social, ethical, and practical considerations. *American Journal of Medicine, 110,* 283–287.

Bandura, A. (1997). *Self-Efficacy: The exercise of control.* New York: Freeman.

Bech, P., Staehr-Johansen, K., & Gudex, C. (1996). The WHO (Ten) Well-Being Index: Validation in diabetes. *Psychotherapy and Psychosomatics, 65,* 183–190.

Caldwell, R. A., Pearson, J. L., & Chin, R. J. (1987). Stress-moderating effects: Social support in the context of gender and locus of control. *Personality and Social Psychology Bulletin, 13,* 5–17.

Cornia, A. G., & Paniccia, R. (2001). *The mortality crisis in transitional economies.* Oxford: Oxford University Press.

Demographic yearbook of Hungary 2002. Budapest: Central Statistical Office.

Dinan, T. G. (1999). Physical consequences of depression. *British Medical Journal, 318,* 826.

Folkman, S., & Lazarus, R. S. (1980). An analysis of coping in a middle aged community sample. *Journal of Health and Social Behavior, 21,* 219–239.

Gárdos, É. (2002). *Health status of population.* Budapest, Hungary: Central Statistical Office.

Glassman, A. H., & Shapiro, P. A. (1998). Depression and the course of coronary artery disease. *American Journal of Psychiatry, 155,* 4–11.

Hemingway, H., & Marmot, M. (1999). Evidence-based cardiology: Psychosocial factors in the aetiology and prognosis of coronary heart disease: Systematic review of prospective cohort studies. *British Medical Journal, 318,* 1460–1467.

Horrobin, D. F., & Bennett, C. N. (1999). Depression and bipolar disorder: Relationships to impaired fatty acid and phospholipid metabolism and to diabetes, cardiovascular disease, immunological abnormalities, cancer, ageing and osteoporosis. *Prostaglandins, Leukocytes and Essential Fatty Acids, 60,* 217–234.

Idler, E. L., & Benyamini, Y. (1997). Self-rated health and mortality: A review of twenty-seven community studies. *Journal of Health and Social Behavior, 38,* 21–37.

Kaplan, G. A., Goldberg, D. E., Everson, S. A., Cohen, R. D., Salonen, R., Tuomilehto, J., & Salonen, J. (1996). Perceived health status and morbidity and mortality: Evidence from the Kuopio Ischemic Heart Disease Risk Factor Study. *International Journal of Epidemiology, 25,* 1–7.

Kielcolt-Glaser, J. K., McGuire, L., Robles, T. F., & Glaser, R. (2002). Emotions, morbidity and mortality: *New Perspectives from Psychoneuroimmunology. 53,* 83–107.

Klinger, A. (2004). Age-standardised midlife (45–64 years) male and female mortality rates in the Hungarian sub-regions in 2001–2003. Report. Budapest, Hungary: Central Statistical Office.

Kopp, M. S., Csoboth, Cs., & Réthelyi, J. (2004a). Psychosocial determinants of premature health deterioration in a changing society: The case of Hungary. *Journal of Health Psychology, 9,* 99–109.

Kopp, M., Falger, P., Appels, A., & Szedmák, S. (1998). Depression and vital exhaustion are differentially related to behavioural risk factors for coronary heart disease. *Psychosomatic Medicine, 60,* 752–758.

Kopp, M. S., & Réthelyi, J. (2004) Where psychology meets physiology: Chronic stress and premature mortality—the Central-Eastern-European health paradox. *Brain Research Bulletin, 62, 351–367.*

Kopp, M. S., Schwarzer, R., & Jerusalem, M. (1993). *Hungarian questionnaire in psychometric scales for cross-cultural self-efficacy research.* Berlin, Germany: Zentrale Universitats Druckerei der FU Berlin.

Kopp, M. S., & Skrabski, Á. (1996). *Behavioural sciences applied to a changing society.* Budapest, Hungary: Biblioteca Septem Artium Liberalium.

Kopp, M. S., Skrabski Á., Réthelyi, J., Kawachi, I., & Adler, N. E. (2004b). Self rated health, subjective social status and middle-aged mortality in a changing society. *Behavioral Medicine, 30*(2), 65–70.

Kopp, M. S., Skrabski, Á., & Szedmák, S. (2000). Psychosocial risk factors, inequality and self-rated morbidity in a changing society. *Social Sciences and Medicine, 51,* 1350–1361.

Kopp, M., Skrabski, Á., & Székely, A. (2002). Risk factors and inequality in relation to morbidity and mortality in a changing society. In G. Weidner, M. S. Kopp, & M. Kristenson (Eds.), *Heart disease: Environment, stress and gender* (pp. 101–113). IOS Press, NATO Science Series, Life and Behavioural Sciences 327.

Kopp, M. S., Szekely, A., & Skarbski, Á. (2004c). Religion and health in a changing society. *Mentálhigiéné és Pszichoszomatika, 5*(2), 103–126. (in Hungarian)

Kubzansky, L. D., & Kawachi, I. (2000): Going to the heart of the matter: Do negative emotions cause coronary heart disease? *Journal of Psychosomatic Research, 48,* 323–337.

Lasa, L., Ayuso-Mateos, J. L., Vazquez-Barquero, J. L., Diez-Manrique, F. J., & Dowrick, C. F. (2000). The use of Beck Depression Inventory to screen for depression in the general population. *Journal of Affective Disorders, 57,* 261–265.

Miilunpalo, S., Vuori, I., Oja, P., Pasanen, M., & Urponen, H. (1997). Self-rated health status as a health measure: The predictive value of self-reported health status on the use of physician services and on mortality in the working age population. *Journal of Clinical Epidemiology, 50,* 517–528.

Miller, W., & Thoresen, C. E. (2003). Spirituality, religion and health: An emerging research field. *American Psychologist, 58,* 24–35.

Moller, L., Kristenson, T. S., & Hollnagel, H. (1996). Self rated health as a predictor of coronary heart disease in Copenhagen, Denmark. *Journal of Epidemiology and Community Health, 50,* 423–428.

Murphy, J. M., Monson, R. R., Olivier, D. C., Sobol, A. M., & Leighton, A. H. (1987). Affective disorders and mortality. *Archives of General Psychiatry, 44,* 473–480.

Musselmann, D. L., Evans, D., & Nemeroff, Ch. B. (1998). The relationship of depression to cardiovascular disease. *Archives of General Psychiatry, 55,* 580–592.

Oman, D, & Thoresen, C. E. (2003). Without spirituality does critical health psychology risk fostering cultural iatrogenesis. *Journal of Health Psychology, 8,* 223–229.

Piko, B. F. (2004). Interplay between self and community: A role for health psychology in Eastern Europe's public health. *Journal of Health Psychology, 9,* 111–120.

Piko, B. F., & Fitzpatrick, K. M. (2004). Substance use, religiosity and other protective factors among Hungarian adolescents. *Addictive Behaviors, 29,* 1095–1107.

Powell, L. H., Shahabi, L., & Thoresen, C. E. (2003). Religion and spirituality: Linkages to physical health. *American Psychologist, 58,* 36–52.

Pratt, L. A., Ford, D. E., Crum, R. M., Armenian, H. K., Gallo, J. J., & Eaton, W. W. (1996). Depression, psychotropic medication and risk of myocardial infarction. Prospective data from the Baltimore ECA follow-up. *Circulation, 94,* 3123–3129.

Rahe, R. H., Taylor, C. B., Tolles, R. T., Newhall, L. M., Veach, T. V., & Bryson, S. (2002). A novel stress and coping workplace program reduces illness and health care utilization. *Psychosomatic Medicine, 64,* 278–286.

Rahe, R. H., & Tolles, R. L. (2002). The Brief Stress and Coping Inventory: A useful stress management instrument. *International Journal of Stress Management, 9*(2), 61–70.

Rahe, R. H., Veach, T. L., Tolles, R. L., & Murakami, K. (2000). The stress and coping inventory: An educational and research instrument. *Stress Medicine, 16,* 199–208.

Rózsa, S., Kő, N., Csoboth, Cs., Purebl, Gy.,5 Beöthy-Molnár, A., Szebik, I., Réthelyi, J., Skrabski, Á., Szádóczky, E., & Kopp, M. (in press). Stress and coping. First results with the Hungarian version of Stress and Coping Questionnaire of Richard Rahe. (Stressz és coping, Elsö eredmények a Stress és coping kérdőív magyar változatával.) *Alkalmazott Pszichológia.*

Rózsa, S., Purebl, Gy., Susánszky, É., Kő, N., Szádóczky, E., Réthelyi, J., Danis, I., Skrabski, Á., & Kopp, M. (in press). Dimensions of coping, Hungarian version of the Ways of Coping Questionnaire. (A coping dimenziói, A Coping kérdőív magyar változata.). *Alkalmazott Pszichológia.*

Rózsa, S., Réthelyi, J., Stauder, A., Susánszky, É., Mészáros, E., Skrabski, Á., & Kopp, M. (2003). The health status of the Hungarian population according to the Hungarostudy 2002: The methods and the characteristics of the representative sample. (A magyar népesség egészségi állapota a Hungarostudy 2002 eredményei szerint: módszerek és a minta jellemzői.) *Psychiatria Hungarica, 18,* 83–94.

Rózsa, S., Szádóczky, E., & Füredi, J. (2001). Psychometric properties of the Hungarian version of the shortened Beck Depression Inventory. (A rövidített Beck Depresszió kérdőív pszichometriai jellemzői.) *Psychiatria Hungarica, 16,* 384–402.

Schwarzer, R. (1993). *Measurement of perceived self-efficacy. Psychometric scales for cross-cultural research.* Berlin, Germany: Freie Universität Berlin.

Seligman, M., & Csikszentmihályi, M. (2000) Positive psychology: An introduction. *American Psychologist, 55,* 5–14.

Skrabski, Á., Kopp, M., & Kawachi, I. (2003). Social capital in a changing society: Cross sectional associations with middle aged female and male mortality rates. *Journal of Epidemiology and Community Health, 57,* 114–119.

Skrabski, Á., Kopp, M., & Kawachi, I. (2004). Social capital and collective efficacy in Hungary: Cross-Sectional associations with middle-aged female and male mortality rates. *Journal of Epidemiology and Community Health, 58,* 340–345.

SPSS. (1999a). *SPSS base 9.0 user's guide.* Chicago: SPSS, Inc.

SPSS. (1999b). *SPSS regression models 9.0.* Chicago: SPSS, Inc.

Wannamethee, G., & Shaper, A. G. (1991). Self-assessment of health status and mortality among middle aged British men. *International Journal of Epidemiology, 20,* 239–245.

World Health Organization. (2001). The world health report, mental health: New understanding, new hope. Geneva: WHO.

International Journal of Behavioral Medicine
2005, Vol. 12, No. 2, 86–97

Dispositional Optimism and the Mechanisms by Which It Predicts Slower Disease Progression in HIV: Proactive Behavior, Avoidant Coping, and Depression

Gail Ironson, Elizabeth Balbin, Rick Stuetzle, Mary Ann Fletcher, Conall O'Cleirigh, J. P. Laurenceau, Neil Schneiderman , and George Solomon

The issue of whether optimism may prospectively protect against disease progression is one that has generated much interest, with mixed results in the literature. The purpose of this study was to determine whether dispositional optimism predicts slower disease progression in HIV. Two indicators of disease progression, CD4 counts and viral load, were assessed over 2 years in a diverse group (men, women, White, African American, Hispanic) of 177 people with HIV in the midrange of disease at entry to the study. Optimism predicted slower disease progression (less decrease in CD4 and less increase in viral load) controlling for baseline CD4 and viral load, antiretroviral treatment, gender, race, education, and drug use. Those low on optimism (25th percentile) lost CD4 cells at a rate 1.55 times faster than those high on optimism (75th percentile). Optimists had higher proactive behavior, less avoidant coping, and less depression: These variables mediated the linear optimism–disease progression relationship. Thus, optimists may reap health benefits partly through behavioral (proactive behavior), cognitive (avoidant coping), and affective (depression) pathways. Implications, limitations, and interpretations are discussed.

Key words: optimism, coping, HIV/AIDS, HIV disease progression, proactive, depression

After years of examining the possible impact of negative factors such as stressful life events, depression, and hostility on disease progression and quality of life after the diagnosis of devastating illnesses, behavioral medicine is now turning its attention to the possible protective effects of positive psychological factors such as meaning, control, and optimism (reviewed in Chesney et al., 2005; Taylor et al., 2000). One of the most intriguing of these is optimism. There is the popular belief that maintaining hope or optimism

may influence survival. Many doctors encourage their patients to develop a positive attitude believing it may be helpful to patients (Schofield et al., 2004). However, there have only been a few studies scientifically examining this.

One study gaining widespread attention (Schofield et al., 2004) recently found that dispositional optimism did not predict progression-free survival in patients with lung cancer and concluded that "encouraging patients to 'be positive' may only add to the burden of having cancer while providing little benefit" (p. 1276). Schulz, Bookwala, Knapp, Scheier, and Williamson (1996) found that, although dispositional optimism did not predict survival in patients with recurrent or metastasized cancer receiving palliative radiation treatment, pessimistic life orientation was a risk factor for mortality but only in younger (age < 59) patients. In contrast, dispositional optimism predicted survival over 1 year in head and neck cancer patients (Allison, Guichard, Fung, & Gilain, 2003). Several studies not restricted to cancer patients found that dispositional optimism is related to better health outcomes including better recovery and less rehospitalization from coronary bypass surgery (Scheier et al., 1989; Scheier et al., 1999) and lower all cause and cardiovascular mortality (Giltay, Geleijnse, Zitman, Hoeskstra, & Evert, 2004).

Gail Ironson, Elizabeth Balbin, Rick Stuetzle, Conall O'Cleirigh, J. P. Laurenceau, Neil Schneiderman, all at the Department of Psychology, University of Miami, Coral Gables, FL 33124–2070, USA; Mary Ann Fletcher, Department of Medicine, University of Miami; George Solomon was Professor Emeritus at the UCLA School of Medicine, Department of Psychiatry and Biobehavioral Medicine, University of California–Los Angeles, Los Angeles, CA 90095–7035, USA.

This research was funded by NIH (R01MH53791 and R01MH066697), principal investigator: Gail Ironson, as well as T32MH18917. Thanks to Kelly Detz for data management; Jeff Gonzalez, Jocelyn Winzer, and Heidemarie Kremer for rating reliability for proactive behavior; and Annie George for conducting many of the interviews.

Correspondence concerning this article should be addressed to Gail Ironson, Department of Psychology, Behavioral Medicine Program, University of Miami, P.O. Box 248185, Coral Gables, FL 33124–2070, USA. E-mail: gironson@aol.com

In addition, one study found that a "cognitive adaptation index," which included dispositional optimism, situational-specific optimism, self-esteem, and mastery, predicted fewer new coronary events after Percutaneous Transluminal Coronary Angioplasty (PTCA) (Helgeson & Fritz, 1999).

Although most of the studies noted previously focused on dispositional optimism (generalized positive expectancies regarding future outcomes; Scheier & Carver, 1985), another approach, optimistic attributional style (Peterson & Seligman, 1984), has also been related to better health across the lifespan (Peterson & Seligman, 1987; Peterson, Seligman, & Vaillant, 1988). An optimistic explanatory style is one that uses attributions for negative events that are external, unstable, and specific rather than internal, stable, and global. This latter type of optimism, however, is only modestly correlated with dispositional optimism. Although the focus of this article is on dispositional optimism, studies of attributional optimism are also noted.

Few studies have been undertaken to determine whether or not optimism prospectively predicts disease progression in HIV. Tomakowsky, Lumley, Markowitz, and Frank (2001) reported unclear results: Dispositional optimism was unrelated to CD4 counts over 2 years, but an optimistic explanatory style was a "substantial" predictor of greater decline in CD4 counts over 2 years. Another study (Reed, Kemeny, Taylor, Wang, & Visscher, 1994) found no association between dispositional optimism and HIV progression. In contrast, optimistic outlook, including anticipating future activities, was related to lower mortality during follow-up in a group of hemophiliacs with HIV (Blomkvist et al., 1994). Dispositional optimism was related to less distress and better cellular immunologic control over Epstein-Barr virus and human herpes virus-6 in the months following Hurricane Andrew in people with HIV (Cruess et al., 2000). An inversely related construct, HIV-specific negative expectancy has been related to earlier symptom onset in bereaved men with HIV (Reed, Kemeny, Taylor, & Visscher, 1999). The most recent study (Milam, Richardson, Marks, Kemper, & McCutchan, 2004) found that dispositional optimism was not linearly related to CD4 or viral load over 18 months; however, optimism had a curvilinear relation with CD4 counts at follow-up (such that moderate levels of optimism at baseline predicted the highest CD4 counts later), and pessimism had a linear relation with higher viral load at follow-up.

In addition to Milam et al.'s (2004) curvilinear findings, the possibility that optimism may not always be beneficial has been suggested by studies of healthy people. For example, Segerstrom (2001) found that optimistic law students had poorer immune status (i.e., lower CD4 cells) when facing academic–social goal conflict. Sieber et al. (1992) found that optimists had a greater decrease in natural killer cell cytotoxicity when exposed to uncontrollable stress (noise). Similarly, F. Cohen et al. (1999) found that optimists showed greater immune decrements than pessimists when stress was maintained at high levels over 3 months. As Segerstrom et al. (2003) note "Optimists' positive moods and confidence" may be "beneficial when coping efforts are effective" but could "lead to greater disappointment and distress when efforts are thwarted or unsuccessful" (p. 1616). These findings suggest that a comprehensive examination of the relation between optimism and immunity should include a consideration of both linear and curvilinear relations.

As Taylor, Kemeny, Reed, Bower, and Gruenewald (2000) note, HIV provides a very useful model for examining psychosocial influences partly because one has meaningful biological markers (CD4 and viral load) to follow and one can control for confounding variables such as age, drug use, sleep, medication use, and so forth. A concern Taylor et al. (2000) raised was whether the discovery of protease inhibitors might limit the use of HIV as a disease model. Most of the studies examining optimism and HIV have been undertaken in samples of men before the advent of powerful medications (protease inhibitors) for HIV. Because of this a statistical modeling procedure, hierarchical linear modeling (HLM; Bryk & Raudenbush, 2002) was selected that allows for the control of time varying covariates (i.e., antiretroviral medication at every time point) and predicts to slope rather than a single point. Thus, the first purpose of this article was to determine whether dispositional optimism would predict disease progression in HIV (both CD4 cell count and HIV-1 viral load) in a diverse sample (e.g., men and women, different ethnic groups) in the era of powerful antiretroviral medications.

A second purpose of this article was to explore mediators of the optimism–disease progression relation. Affective, cognitive, and behavioral pathways were considered. Several studies have shown, for example, that optimism prospectively predicts a resistance to the development of depression and better emotional recovery in various medical populations including women undergoing breast cancer surgery (Carver et al., 1993; Schou et al., 2004) and patients undergoing treatment for metastatic melanoma and renal cell carcinoma (L. Cohen et al., 2001). Optimism has also been related cross-sectionally to less distress in men with HIV (Taylor et al., 1992). Thus, one plausible mechanism by which optimism could impact on disease progression is by resistance to negative emotional states such as depression. Depression, in turn, has been shown to predict disease progression in a number of studies (see Leserman, 2003, for a review).

A second pathway by which optimism could impact CD4, viral load change, or both is through coping. Optimism has been positively related to active coping efforts (Aspinwall & Taylor, 1992; Taylor et al., 1992). These efforts may in turn mitigate the effect of the stressor both affectively and physiologically. Furthermore, optimists persist in goal attainment even in the face of obstacles (Carver & Scheier, 1998). As noted in Segerstrom, Taylor, Kemeny, and Fahey (1998), dispositional optimists make less use of avoidant coping strategies such as denial and giving up, which have been associated with negative affect (Taylor et al., 1992) and the development of symptoms and death in HIV (Ironson et al., 1994).

Health behaviors could also provide a connection between optimism and health (Mulkana & Hailey, 2001). In men at risk for HIV, Taylor et al. (1992) showed that men who were unrealistically optimistic about their ability to stave off the HIV virus nonetheless practiced better health habits. However, they found that there was no relation of optimism to risk-related sexual behavior. In contrast, Holmes and Pace (2002) found that optimistic beliefs about prognosis were significantly related to both poor medication adherence and risky sex. Finally, drug use and sleep could also be plausible pathways by which optimism could affect immune function (Kiecolt-Glaser & Glaser, 1988) and disease progression and were examined as potential mediators.

Thus, this article seeks to examine whether dispositional optimism predicts HIV disease progression and what the mediators of this relation might be. It extends previous literature by having a more diverse sample (30% women, 70% men), predicting to both CD4 and viral load, being undertaken in an era when powerful medications are available, controlling for medications at every time point, and examining possible mechanisms. Finally, both linear and nonlinear prediction are considered.

Methods

Participants

Inclusion criteria. Participants were HIV positive with CD4 counts between 150 and 500 at entry to the study (chosen so they were in the midrange of illness when one starts to get symptoms).

Exclusion criteria. Participants were excluded if they had ever had an AIDS-defining symptom (Category C symptoms such as Kaposi's sarcoma, *Pneumocystis carinii* pneumonia, etc.), had ever had CD4 cell count below 75, were younger than 18 years, had another life-threatening illness (e.g., cancer), were taking medications thought to affect stress hormones (e.g., steroids, propranolol), were actively psychotic or suicidal, were having current alcohol or drug dependence (based on the psychotic screen and alcohol and drug use modules from the Structured Clinical Interview Diagnosis for the American Psychiatric Association *Diagnostic and Statistical Manual of Mental Disorders,* 3rd ed., rev.), had less than an eighth-grade education in English, or had dementia.

Design

This is a longitudinal study in which participants were seen at five time points (every 6 months for 2 years). Accrual lasted 2.5 years. The time period was between 1997 and 2002.

Procedures

At the initial visit, we obtained informed consent and participants were given a questionnaire packet (described in the measures section). They also underwent an interview, which assessed background information, current life stress, questions about the development of new symptoms, medication, and an assessment of exclusion variables (e.g., drug and alcohol dependence, psychotic screen, and cognitive status as noted previously). They also underwent a blood draw for CD4 and viral load and a brief physical examination to check for the development of Category C symptoms. Blood draws were conducted in the morning to control for diurnal variation. Participants were thanked for their time and paid $50. Similar assessment procedures were followed at each of the 6-month follow-up time points.

Measures

Demographics. Demographics included age, gender (1 = male, 0 = female), ethnicity (1 = White, 0 = other), sexual orientation (1 = heterosexual, 0 = gay/bisexual), and socioeconomic status (SES; education, employment, income). Education was used to represent SES in the HLM models, because it cannot be affected by disease whereas employment and income may be. Education was assessed as less than high school; high school or more, but less than college degree; or college graduate or more.

Background medical information. Background medical information includes CD4 count, viral load, prescribed antiretroviral medications, route of infection, and additional (possibly control, possibly predictor) variables that could affect the course of HIV (including past history of sexually transmitted diseases, sleep, alcohol and drug use, adherence to medication, exercise). Antiretrovirals were dummy coded at each time point reflecting three levels: no medication, combination therapy, or highly active antiretroviral treatment (HAART, which during this study period was combination therapy including a protease inhibitor or Ziagen [abacavir], Sustiva [favirenz], or Viread [tenofovir]).

Disease progression markers. Peripheral blood samples were collected from all participants in ethyl-enediaminetetraacetic acid (EDTA) tubes (Vacutainer EDTA, Becton-Dickenson, Rytherford, NJ). The percentage of CD4 lymphocytes (CD3+, CD4+) was determined by whole-blood four-color direct immuno-fluorescence using a Coulter XL-MCL flow cytometer (Coulter Epics XL-MCL, Miami, FL) in line with the method described by Fletcher, Maher, Patarca, and Klimas (2000). Lymphocyte counts were determined using a Beckman/Coulter Hmx hematology analyzer (Beckman/Coulter, Hialeah, FL). The CD4 count was the product of the lymphocyte count and the percentage of lymphocytes positive for both CD4+ and CD3+ markers. Viral load was determined on EDTA plasma using an *in vitro* reverse transcriptase polymerase chain reaction assay (Amplicor, Roche Laboratories, Indianapolis, IN). Results were expressed as HIV-1 ribonucleic acid (RNA) copies per milliliter. A log transformation was used to normalize the distribution.

Psychosocial measures. Optimism was measured by a composite of the Life Orientation Test (LOT; Scheier & Carver, 1985) and the LOT-R (Scheier, Carver, & Bridges, 1994), which assess dispositional optimism or the extent to which one generally anticipates positive outcomes (e.g., I always look on the bright side of things). Participants were asked the degree to which they agreed with each of nine substantive statements (and one filler, not scored) on a scale from 1 to 4. This scale differs from the often used 5-point scale because it does not have a neutral (neither agree nor disagree) option. Higher scores represent higher optimism. Depression was measured by the Beck Depression Inventory (BDI; A. T. Beck, 1967; Beckman & Leber, 1985). Perceived stress was measured by the Perceived Stress Scale (PSS; 10-item version; S. Cohen & Williamson, 1988), which measures "the degree to which situations in one's life are appraised as stressful." Coping was measured by the COPE (Carver, Scheier, & Weintraub, 1989). Two subscales were combined to produce an avoidant coping composite (denial and behavioral disengagement). An adaptive coping composite was also constructed (via factor analysis) from five subscales—planning, positive reframing, active coping, acceptance, and emotional support.

Behaviors. Adherence was measured by the proportion of missed doses by self-report on the AIDS Clinical Trial Group (ACTG) adherence measure (Chesney et al., 2000). Drug and alcohol use in the past

month were assessed by self-report using a 5-point Likert scale (no use, once or twice, once a week, several times a week, or daily) for the following substances: alcohol, cigarettes, marijuana, and cocaine. Sleep and exercise were assessed through self-report asking "How much sleep did you get each night during the past week?" and the number of hours of physical exercise during the past week. Safe sex was measured by reported use of condoms (for those who were sexually active). Proactive behavior was measured by ratings from interviews. The interviewer asked a variety of questions, the most relevant of which are how the research participant has been dealing with HIV, what he or she is doing to keep healthy, and whether he or she is satisfied with the doctor. Proactive behavior included reports of self-initiated action-oriented behavior. Examples included information seeking, changing a health behavior, seeking medical care, seeking another doctor's opinion, refusing to be a victim or fighting spirit, and seeking mental health and substance abuse counseling. Reliability for this scoring system between two raters ($n = 21$) scoring written material was $r = .86$ (K.D. and H.M.K.). A subset of 15 participant interviews were also rated by blind raters (J.G. and J.W.) yielding an r of .66, $p = .007$; Kendall's τ-b of .53, $T = 2.869$, $p = .004$. In only 1 of the 15 participants did the ratings (done on a scale of 0 to 3) differ by more than 1.

Statistical Methods

The main analyses used HLM (Bryk & Raudenbush, 2002) to predict CD4 and viral load change over time. Key features that led to the choice to use this technique for analysis were that it allows one to control for antiretroviral use at each time point, it allows one to predict to slope of change rather than a single endpoint, and it allows one to calculate the expected drop in CD4 cells (or increase in viral load) over a period of time for any given score of a psychological variable. In this data analytic approach, variance in disease progression markers is separated into two levels. Level 1 represents a growth model for each individual capturing within-person change in CD4 and (log) viral load over repeated measurements. Level 2 represents a model of interindividual differences in parameters of individual change and uses between-person characteristics such as education and psychological variables to predict change. Thus, systematic variability of slopes and intercepts at Level 1 are modeled by predictors at Level 2.

Covariate Selection

A priori variables controlled for included initial disease status (CD4 and viral load at study entry—controlled through the intercept in the HLM model), prescribed treatment (antiretrovirals as a time-dependent covariate), and time since entry into the study. Other covariates that were considered based on prior HIV literature (Balbin, Ironson, & Solomon, 1999; Ickovics et al., 2001, Leserman et al., 2000) included demographics (race, gender, age, SES; education was used because it is not affected by HIV as income and employment are) and background variables relevant to HIV (sexual orientation, route of infection) or that impact on the immune system (Kiecolt-Glaser & Glaser, 1988; drug and alcohol use in past month, smoking, exercise, sleep). Covariates were tested individually after controlling for antiretrovirals, baseline health status, and time since entry to the study. Those covariates having $p < .10$ were kept in the model and tested simultaneously. Those still significant at $p < .10$ were kept in the resulting model. Covariates that had been excluded were then retested with all other significant covariates to determine if they should be reentered. After determination of covariates, the final models added optimism as a Level 2 predictor.

Of additional note, recognizing the possibility that health status might affect optimism suggests that optimism should perhaps be controlled for in the intercept at Level 2. However, the correlation between initial CD4 count and optimism was not significant ($r = -.02$) nor was the correlation between optimism and initial viral load ($r = .06$).

All continuous variables in the model were centered and all categorical variables were coded with zero as the lowest level. HLM parameter estimates account for missingness on the outcome variables by using full maximum likelihood estimation. The log of viral load was used rather than absolute amount as the variable was skewed.

The two level equations including significant covariates are detailed in Table 1 (with optimism in the model) and summarized as follows.

For CD4

Level 1: $Yti = \beta_{0i} + \beta_{1i}$(months since baseline)$_{ti}$ + β_{2i}(antiretroviral 1)$_{ti}$ + β_{3i}(antiretroviral 2)$_{ti}$ + β_{4i}(antiretroviral 1 × time)$_{ti}$ + β_{5i}(antiretroviral 2 × time)$_{ti}$ + e_{ti}

where Yti is the CD4 count for participant i at time point t,

β_{0i} is CD4 at entry to the study for the ith participant,

β_{1i} is the slope representing linear change in CD4 over time for participant i,

β_{2i}, β_{3i}, β_{4i}, β_{5i} are the slopes for the antiretrovirals (two variables dummy coded representing the three levels of medication—none, combination therapy, or HAART) and the interaction of antiretrovirals and months since baseline,

e_{ti} is a residual term for participant i at time t.

To examine individual differences in Level 1 change parameters, the Level 2 equations are as follows:

β_{01} (intercept) = $\gamma_{00} + \gamma_{01}$ (gender)$_i$ + γ_{02} (ethnicity-white/not)$_i$ + u_0

β_{1i} (slope) = $\gamma_{10} + \gamma_{11}$(education)$_i$ + γ_{12}(marijuana use)$_i$ + γ_{13}(optimism) + u_1

$\beta_{2i,3i} = \gamma_{20,30}$(antiretroviral 1 or 2),

$\beta_{4i,5i} = \gamma_{40,50}$(antiretroviral 1 or 2 × time)

where γ_{00} represents the group average initial CD4,

γ_{10} represents the average linear change in CD4,

γ_{20} and γ_{30} represent the average effect on level of CD4 across patients of being on antiretroviral 1 or 2 (two dummy coded variables representing three levels of medication—none, combination therapy, or HAART) on level of CD4,

γ_{40} and γ_{50} represent the average effect across patients of antiretroviral 1 and antiretroviral 2 on change in CD4 over time,

γ_{13} represents the effect of individual differences on CD4 slope (γ_{10}) attributable to putative psychological variables beyond the effect of other covariates in the model.

For viral load

Level 1: $Yti = \beta_{01} + \beta_{1i}$(months since baseline)$_{ti}$ + β_{2i}(antiretroviral 1)$_{ti}$ + β_{3i}(antiretroviral 2)$_{ti}$ + e_{ti}

To examine individual differences in Level 1 change parameters, the Level 2 equations are as follows:

β_{01}(intercept) = $\gamma_{00} + \gamma_{01}(age)_i$ + γ_{02}(gender)$_i$ + γ_{03}(cocaine use)$_i$ + u_0

β_{1i} (slope) = $\gamma_{10} + \gamma_{11}$(education)$_i$ + γ_{12}(sexual orientation)$_i$ + γ_{13}(optimism) + u_1

$\beta_{2i,3i} = \gamma_{20}, \gamma_{30}$ (antiretroviral 1 or 2)

where Yti is the viral load (log) for participant i at time point t,

β_{0i} is viral load (log) at baseline for the ith participant,

β_{1i} is the slope representing linear change in viral load over time for participant i,

e_{ti} is the residual or random error term associated with time point t for participant I,

u represents random error associated with estimation of the B coefficients,

β_{2i} and β_{3i} are the average effects across patients being on antiretroviral 1 and antiretroviral 2, respectively.

Table 1a. *HLM Model Including Coefficients and Significance Tests for Level 1 and Level 2 Covariates and Optimism in Prediction of CD4 Slope Over 2 Years, Controlling for Retained Covariates*

Fixed Effect	Coefficient	Standard Error	t ratio	df	p value
CD4 intercept, β_0					
Average initial CD4, γ_{00}	296.31	17.84	16.61	174	<.001
Gender, γ_{01}	−34.42	17.11	−2.01	174	.044
Ethnicity, γ_{02}	38.62	16.10	2.40	174	.017
CD4 slope (per month), β_1					
Average slope, γ_{10}	−3.13	0.83	−2.46	173	.014
Education, γ_{11}	1.01	0.76	1.34	173	.181
Marijuana use, γ_{12}	−1.07	0.37	−2.90	173	.004
Optimism, γ_{13}	0.19	0.09	2.08	173	.037
Antiretroviral 1 increment, β_2					
Average increment, γ_{20}	48.53	16.75	2.90	718	.004
Antiretroviral 2 increment β_3					
Average increment γ_{30}	18.00	14.05	1.28	718	.200
Antiretroviral 1 increment over time, β_4					
Average increment over time, γ_{40}	3.11	1.36	2.28	718	.022
Antiretroviral 2 increment over time, β_5					
Average increment over time, γ_{50}	3.33	0.94	3.53	718	.001

Note. HLM = hierarchical linear modeling.

Table 1b. *Prediction of log Viral Load Slope Over 2 Years From Optimism Controlling for Retained Covariates*

Fixed Effect	Coefficient	Standard Error	t ratio	df	p value
VL log intercept, β_0					
Intercept, γ_{00}	4.567	0.140	32.67	173	< .001
Age, γ_{01}	−0.014	0.008	−1.85	173	.064
Gender, γ_{02}	−0.288	0.157	−1.84	173	.066
Cocaine use, γ_{03}	0.197	0.094	2.08	173	.037
VL log slope (per month), β_1					
Average slope, γ_{10}	0.013	0.004	2.98	173	.003
Education, γ_{11}	−0.007	0.004	−1.51	173	.130
Sexual orientation, γ_{12}	−0.016	0.006	−2.63	173	.009
Optimism, γ_{13}	−0.001	.001	−2.01	173	.044
Antiretroviral 1 increment, β_2					
Average increment, γ_{20}	−0.997	0.120	−8.29	719	< .001
Antiretroviral 2 increment, β_3					
Average increment, γ_{20}	−1.032	0.112	−9.25	719	< .001

Note. VL = viral load.

Results

Description of the Sample

Our sample (*N* = 177) was diverse: 30% female, 70% male; 31% white, 36% African American, 28% Hispanic, and 5% other. The average age was 37.5, and the SES was low to moderate (62% make less than $10,000/year; 27% are college graduates). Thirty-six percent had a history of alcohol abuse, 31% had a history of cocaine abuse, and 24% had a history of *Cannabis* abuse. Fifty-one percent obtained HIV from gay or bisexual sex, 38% from heterosexual sex, 5% from intravenous drug use, and the rest from multiple or other sources. At entry to the study, the average CD4 was 296.7 (*SD* =102.45), and average viral load was 44,861. Seventy-seven percent were on antiretroviral medications (56.5% were on HAART). Complete details of the demographics and

medical information for the sample are given in Ironson et al. (2005).

Optimism and Disease Progression

Table 1a presents the HLM model with significant covariates for the prediction of CD4 slope over 2 years, and Table 1b presents the HLM model for the prediction of viral load (log). As can be seen, there was a significant decrease in CD4 over time, and a significant increase in viral load (log). Controlling for significant covariates, optimism measured at baseline predicts the change in CD4 (slope) over 2 years: γ_{13} = 0.19, *t* = 2.08, *df* = 173, *p* = .04. Although the sample as a whole loses 3.13 CD4 cells per month,[1] optimists

---

[1]The average decline in CD4 cells of 3.13 per month is estimated using γ_{13} based on average scores on the continuous variables and zero on the categorical variables, controlling for the covariates in the model.

gain 0.19 CD4 cells per month for every one point on the LOT. For example, the sample as a whole loses $3.13 \times 12 = 37.56$ CD4 cells per year. A high optimist who is 3.8 points above the mean on the LOT (at the 75th percentile) would gain $0.19 \times 3.8 = .72$ CD4 cells per month or 8.67 CD4 cells per year above the -37.56 for the sample as a whole for a total loss of only 28.89 CD4 cells a year. A low optimist, on the other hand (at the 25th percentile) is 3.2 points below the mean and would lose an additional $-0.19 \times 3.2 = -0.61$ CD4 cells per month or 7.32 CD4 cells per year above the -37.56 for the sample as a whole, which translates into a decline of 44.88 CD4 cells per year. The decline ratio for low versus high optimists may then be calculated to be 44.88/28.89 or 1.55. Thus, low optimists lose 55% more CD4 cells per year than high optimists. Optimism also predicts the change in viral load (log) over time: $\gamma_{13} = -0.001$, $t = -2.007$, $df = 173$, $p = .04$. In this case, high optimists have a slower increase in viral load (log) over time compared to low optimists.

Correlates of Optimism

The first step in exploring possible mediators of the relation between optimism and disease progression was to determine which of our hypothesized mediators were significantly correlated with optimism. Three types of variables were considered: (a) mood/affect (BDI, PSS); (b) coping (avoidant, adaptive); and (c) behaviors, which included safe sex (condom use if sexually active), adherence to medications, drug use (marijuana, cocaine, alcohol, cigarette smoking), exercise, sleep, and proactive behavior. Optimism was significantly correlated with these psychosocial variables: depression ($r = -.66$, $p < .01$), perceived stress ($r = -.62$, $p < .01$), avoidant coping ($r = -.29$, $p < .01$), and adaptive coping ($r = .44$, $p < .01$). In addition, optimism was significantly correlated with these behaviors: adherence ($r = .18$, $p < .05$), cocaine use ($r = -.28$, $p < .01$), cigarette smoking ($r = -.22$, $p < .01$), exercise

($r = .17$, $p < .05$), and proactive behavior ($r = .26$, $p < .01$). Optimism was not significantly related to practicing safe sex ($r = .06$), alcohol use ($r = .01$), or sleep ($r = .12$).

Mediator Analysis

In addition to being related to optimism, several other criteria as outlined in Baron and Kenny (1986) need to be met. That is, the putative mediator must also predict the outcome variable (CD4 or viral load change), and when both the mediator and optimism are in the equation together, the mediator remains significant and optimism is no longer significant. For partial mediation, optimism is still significant, but the path from optimism to disease progression is reduced in absolute size—optimism explains less of the variance in the dependent variable/disease progression—when the putative mediator is controlled (i.e., added into the equation) compared to when optimism was a predictor without the mediator. Table 2 has the previously mentioned analyses for testing for prediction and mediation (i.e., Table 2 includes only variables correlating with optimism, as noted in the previous paragraph, that also predicted either CD4 or viral load change). The last column, the Sobel test (Sobel, 1982), tests whether a mediator carries the influence of an Independent Variable (IV) to a Dependent Variable (DV) (Preacher & Leonardelli, 2003) or, more precisely, whether the indirect effect of the IV on the DV via the mediator is significantly different from zero.

Mediators of optimism to CD4 change. As can be seen from Table 2, depression was the first variable to qualify as a mediator as it predicts CD4 change, and when both optimism and depression are in the model, depression continues to predict but optimism does not. (Note that examined the other way around, optimism was not a mediator of the depression–disease progression relation.) Finally, the Sobel test was significant. Proactive behavior also mediated the relationship be-

Table 2. *Mediator Analysis for Potential Mediators (Measured at Baseline) That Predict CD4 or VL Change*

Mediator	Mediator Alone *t*	Mediator Controlling for Optimism *t*	Optimism Controlling for Mediator *t*	Sobel Test |z|
Prediction to CD4 slope				
Depression (BDI)	−2.814**	−2.201*	0.352	2.163*
Avoidant coping	−1.855+	−1.418	1.591	1.335
Proactive behavior	3.470**	3.140**	1.636+	2.312*
Prediction to VL(log) slope				
Depression (BDI)	3.358**	2.850**	0.251	2.443*
Avoidant coping	3.097**	2.718**	−1.382	2.171*
Denial	2.245*	2.034*	−1.715+	1.411
Behavioral disengagement	2.881**	2.359*	−1.343	2.122*
Proactive behavior	−0.592	−0.224	−1.835+	0.218

Note. BDI = Beck Depression Inventory; VL = viral load.
*$p < .05$. **$p < .01$. +$p < .10$.

tween optimism and CD4 change. Finally, avoidant coping was not a mediator.

One might argue that true mediation should involve measurement of the mediator at a later time point. Because of this, the mediator analyses were repeated with measurement of the mediators at Time 2 (6 months after baseline assessment). These analyses are presented in Table 3 and illustrate that the findings hold for depression and proactive behavior. Furthermore, avoidant coping emerged as a significant mediator when it was measured at Time 2.

Mediators of optimism to viral load change. Similarly, depression qualifies as a mediator because it predicts viral load (log) change, and when both optimism and depression are in the model, depression continues to predict but optimism does not. As before, the Sobel test is significant. Avoidant coping also mediated the relation between optimism and viral load (log) change. Follow-up analyses examining denial and behavioral disengagement separately suggested that behavioral disengagement was the subscale that was driving this effect more powerfully. Proactive coping did not mediate the optimism–viral load relation. As before, one might argue that true mediation should involve measurement of the mediator at a later time point. Because of this, the mediator analyses were repeated with measurement of the mediators at Time 2. These analyses are presented in Table 3 and illustrate that the findings hold for depression. However, they did not hold for avoidant coping or proactive behavior.

Exploration of curvilinear relations. Based on the findings of Milam et al. (2004), further analyses were undertaken to determine whether there was a curvilinear relation between optimism and either CD4 or viral load. When the quadratic term for optimism was entered into the model with the other covariates plus linear optimism in the model, there were nonsignificant trends for the quadratic optimism term to predict viral load ($t_{172} = -1.86$, $p = .06$) and CD4 ($t_{172} = 1.59$, $p = .11$).

Discussion

Dispositional optimism predicts two markers of HIV disease progression in an era when very potent antiretrovirals are available and in a very diverse sample. Further analyses suggest that optimism may be related to disease progression through several mediators: more proactive behavior, less depression, and less avoidant coping. Thus, optimists may reap health benefits partly through behavioral (proactive behavior), cognitive (avoidant coping), and affective (depression) pathways. In other words, maintaining a positive outlook may serve to keep people more behaviorally engaged and less avoidant (i.e., better able to face the facts) and may confer resistance to depression.

Correlates and Mediators

Consistent with other studies, we found significant relations between optimism and affective variables, such as depression, and with avoidant and adaptive coping, but no relation between optimism and sexual behavior was observed. Less studied are relations between optimism and adherence to medications, drug use (marijuana, cocaine, alcohol, cigarette smoking), exercise, sleep, and proactive behavior. In our sample, optimism was significantly correlated with many of these behaviors: adherence, exercise, cocaine use (negatively), and cigarette smoking (negatively), but none of these met the criteria for mediation. Finally, one new variable that optimism was both related to and met the criteria for a mediator of the optimism–disease progression relation is proactive behavior. Thus, this study extends the literature by showing not only associations but also that proactive behavior, depression, and avoidant coping are mediators of the optimism–disease progression relation.

Although the optimism–proactive behavior–disease progression relation is relatively new, it is consistent with the literature. Carver and Scheier (1998) suggest that optimists are more likely to persist toward goal attainment even in the face of obstacles or stressors. In one study, optimists remained more persistent on a vig-

Table 3. *Mediator Analysis for Potential Mediators (Measured at Time 2) That Predict CD4 or VL Change*

Mediator	Mediator Alone *t*	Mediator Controlling for Optimism *t*	Optimism Controlling for Mediator *t*	Sobel Test |z|
Prediction to CD4 slope				
Depression	−3.960**	−2.969**	1.300	2.487*
Avoidant coping	−3.387**	−2.448*	1.340	2.145*
Proactive behavior	3.383**	3.054**	1.675	1.987*
Prediction to VL (log) slope				
Depression	4.055**	3.379**	−0.876	2.714*
Avoidant coping	2.129*	1.212	−1.273	1.169
Proactive behavior	−1.246	−0.916	−1.597	0.865

Note. VL = viral load.
*$p < .05$. **$p < .01$.

ilance task than pessimists even when given false-negative feedback (Helton, Dember, Warm, & Matthews, 1999). The literature reviewed by Segerstrom, Castañeda, and Spencer (2003) suggest that optimists may have an easier time persisting with controllable rather than uncontrollable stressors, situations in which there is not goal conflict, and situations in which coping efforts make a difference. Since the advent of powerful medications for HIV, the management of this illness has become more controllable, and coping efforts can make a difference. In addition, Scheier and Carver (1987) suggest that pessimists are more emotion focused under stress than optimists, which would also be consistent with a prediction that optimists would remain more problem focused and perhaps more proactive. In the long run, this disposition could lead to better health management. Thus, optimists may be more action oriented despite the stresses in life. This interpretation would also be consistent with learned helplessness theory such that optimists may have had more responsive early learning environments and have learned that persistence and proactive behavior are more likely to be rewarded (Peterson & Seligman, 1987; Peterson et al., 1988).

Depression was also identified as a mediator of the relation between optimism and disease progression. Thus, optimism appears to act at least partially via depression. Other investigators have raised the question of whether measures of depression and optimism are distinct from each other (Smith et al., 1989) or may both reflect underlying negative affectivity or neuroticism. Although this is one possible interpretation of the high correlation between optimism and depression found in this ($r = -.66$) and other studies, another interpretation is that depression is a conceptually distinct but highly correlated construct. The measure of depression used in this study was the BDI, which assesses several domains: cognitive, affective, and somatic symptoms across 21 items (A. Beck, Ward, Mendelsohn, Mock, & Erbaugh, 1961). The only item that can be directly thought to be measuring the same construct (inversely) as optimism is the hopelessness item (e.g., I feel discouraged about the future). In addition, the BDI assesses depressive symptoms over the previous week, whereas the time frame on the LOT is not specified but rather refers to a generalized "way of looking at life." Related to this, depression can be conceptualized as a state measure thought to be more amenable to change (Vos et al., 2004) as compared with dispositional optimism, which is thought to be more of a trait measure. Second, one would expect depression and optimism to be highly correlated because the literature on depression suggests that negative, nonoptimistic thinking is part of the problem that depressed people have (Beck, 1967). Similarly, optimism may confer a resistance to depression. Third, the two variables performed differently in the mediator analysis:

Optimism was not a mediator of the depression–disease progression relation (see Tables 2 and 3). In conclusion, there may well be areas of shared variance among optimism, trait neuroticism, and depression; however, depression, assessed via the BDI, measures state depression, and our data suggest one legitimate possibility is to view depression as a mediator of the optimism–disease progression relation. Although our data are supportive of this interpretation, to establish a true mediator causality rather than prospective correlational analysis (even using an intervening time point) needs to be demonstrated.

Reconciliation With Other HIV Literature

Our study findings are consistent with the Blomkvist et al. (1994) study, in which optimistic outlook and anticipating future activities was related to lower mortality during follow-up in a group of hemophiliacs. However, the findings of this study contrast with the Tomakowsky et al. (2001) study that did not find a relationship of dispositional optimism to CD4 change, the Milam et al. (2004) study that did not find a linear relationship between optimism and CD4, and the Reed et al. (1994) study that did not find a relationship to survival time. There are several possible reasons for these discrepancies: Most importantly, in all three negative studies the linear contribution of optimism was tested after controlling for important psychological variables such as negative affectivity (in Tomakowsky et al.), depression (in Milam et al.), and coping (in Reed et al.) that were conceptualized in this study as potential mediators. (Note that in our study, see Table 2, the linear prediction from optimism is no longer predictive if one controls for depression, which is a variable related to negative affectivity or if one controls for avoidant coping.) Second, there were differences in other covariates, for example, the Tomakowsky et al. study controlled only for whether or not the patient was taking zidovudine (likely because that was the only relevant medication at the time), and the Milam et al. study included only patients on Antiretroviral Therapy (ART), whereas this study controlled more specifically for type of medication (none, combination therapy, HAART) and did so at every time point. Our study also controlled for recreational drug use (marijuana and cocaine). In addition, our study used the same laboratory for all CD4 and viral load measurements, whereas the Milam et al. study used medical records, which may have introduced method variance. Fourth, there were differences in the samples: Two studies followed only men and one study followed predominantly men (Milam et al., 88% men), whereas ours followed a diverse group of men and women. In addition, the sample sizes differed ($n = 47$ in Tomakowsky et al., $n = 78$ in the Reed et al. study, $n = 177$ in our study, and $n = 412$

in the Milam et al. study). Another important difference is that our sample was restricted to those in the midrange of HIV at study entry (our sample was restricted to those with CD4 counts between 150 and 500 at baseline) where we hypothesized that the impact of psychological variables would not be overwhelmed by advanced biological deterioration. Finally, in view of these discrepant results (which may in fact, not be all that discrepant as noted previously), more studies need to be conducted to reconcile these results.

Our study also contrasts with the study of lung cancer patients in which optimism did not predict disease course (Schofield et al., 2004) and in patients with metastasized and recurrent cancer (Schulz et al., 1996). One possible reason for a discrepancy is that certain diseases may be more amenable to psychological influences than others. In addition, as noted previously, psychological factors may play a more prominent role at certain stages of a disease, that is, before the biological deterioration is overwhelming. If one's model hypothesizes that psychological variables impact on disease course through the immune and endocrine systems, then cancers that are immunogenic (e.g., melanoma) or virally mediated (e.g., cervical cancer) would be more likely illnesses to find a psychological effect on disease course. Similarly, because the immune system is involved in HIV, and HIV is a virus, there are plausible biological pathways by which psychological factors such as optimism could have an impact.

Curvilinear Associations

Both our study and the Milam et al. (2004) study tested the curvilinear association between optimism and disease progression. We did not find a significant curvilinear relation between optimism and disease progression markers although there was a nonsignificant trend for viral load. Although this result is not definitive, the finding of trends suggests that further exploration of curvilinear models is warranted. It should be noted that the Milam et al. study had a larger sample size, and thus more power, and used different covariates. Most notably the Milam et al. model controlled for depression, which we did not do; we controlled for drugs and three levels of antiretroviral medications changing at every time point.

Limitations and Future Directions

It should be noted that this study only measured dispositional optimism (Scheier & Carver, 1985) and not attributional optimism. As noted, dispositional optimism focuses on generalized positive expectancies regarding future outcomes and is derived from behavioral self-regulation theory. The other approach, formulated by Peterson and Seligman (1984), was derived from the reformulated learned helplessness model and

focuses on optimism as an explanatory style. An optimistic explanatory style is one that uses attributions for negative events that are external, unstable, and specific rather than internal, stable, and global.

In addition, this article did not address the chicken or egg question. That is, does optimism lead to continued good health, or does continued good health lead to optimism? This is left for future research and should be answered making a conceptual distinction between dispositional and attributional optimism, because the latter may be more amenable to change. A further question that this study did not address that would be helpful for future studies to address is distinguishing between realistic optimism and unrealistic optimism. Unfortunately, this is hard to define, although not impossible in HIV because there are prognostic disease progression markers.

As suggested previously, further research should identify which diseases and at what point in the course of the disease optimism would be protective of health and immunity. In addition, we did not address the question of the unique effects of optimism versus pessimism. Finally, the results of the curvilinear analyses deserve more attention because the findings showed a nonsignificant trend.

Implications for Clinical Practice

Should doctors tell their patients to maintain a positive outlook? Our results suggest that having a positive, optimistic attitude may be helpful due to its relation with slower disease progression. Mediational analyses suggest that encouraging people to be more proactive, helping them to be less avoidant, and screening and treating them for depression could contribute to some of the protective effects of optimism as well.

On the flip side, unrealistic optimism is likely to be deleterious. As Peterson and Vaidya (2003) note "Optimism is suspect if it leads to pointless persistence" (p. 33). A more useful strategy may be to follow what Seligman (1991) called "flexible optimism" or what Armor and Taylor (1998) call "strategic optimism," which is a psychological strategy to be exercised when appropriate.

A study suggesting optimism is related to disease progression raises another question: What can be done to raise optimism levels, or, said differently, what can be done to help people maintain hope? Seligman (1991) has written about learned optimism, but how much of this applies or would be useful in a medical situation is unknown. This study has also not addressed the question of whether a doctor-suggested optimistic attitude would make a difference. Furthermore, as noted, the data suggest that one may confer some of the benefits of optimism by encouraging proactive behavior and by preventing depression and avoidant coping. This may be easier and more realistic than trying to impact on dispositional optimism, which may in fact be more of a trait and may have resulted from years of learning and conditioning (and conversely from learned helplessness) or even partially from a genetic predisposition (Schulman, Keith, & Seligman, 1993), neither of which are easy to change. The issue of how much one should encourage patients to be optimistic for other reasons (i.e., quality of life) is beyond the scope of this article but is nonetheless important. Similarly, issues surrounding the fine line of giving enough hope to patients to help them function and enjoy life versus giving them false hope needs to include much more than the statistical findings available from this article.

References

Allison, P. J., Guichard C., Fung, K., & Gilain, L. (2003). Dispositional optimism predicts survival status 1 year after diagnosis in head and neck cancer patients. *Journal of Clinical Oncology, 21,* 543–548.

American Psychiatric Association. (1987). *Diagnostic and statistical manual of mental disorders.* (3rd ed., rev.). Washington, DC: Author.

Armor, D. A., & Taylor, S. E. (1998). Situated optimism: Specific outcome expectancies and self-regulation. *Advances in Experimental Social Psychology, 30,* 309–379.

Aspinwall, L. G., & Taylor, S. E. (1992). Individual differences, coping, and psychological adjustment: A longitudinal study of college adjustment and performance. *Journal of Personality and Social Psychology, 63,* 989–1003.

Balbin, E. G., Ironson, G. H., & Solomon, G. F. (1999). Stress and coping: The psychoneuroimmunology of HIV/AIDS. *Best Practical Research Clinical Endocrinology & Metabolism, 13,* 615–633.

Baron, R. M., & Kenny, D. A. (1986). The moderator-mediator variable distinction is social psychological research: Conceptual, strategic, and statistical considerations. *Journal of Personality and Social Psychology, 56,* 267–283.

Beck, A., Ward, C., Mendelsohn, M., Mock, J., & Erbaugh, J. (1961). An inventory for measuring depression. *Archives of General Psychiatry, 4,* 561–571.

Beck, A. T. (1967). *Depression: Causes and treatment.* Philadelphia: University of Pennsylvania Press.

Beckman, E. E., & Leber, W. R. (Eds.). (1985). *Handbook of depression: Treatment, assessment, and research* (Appendix 3). Homewood, IL: Dorsey.

Blomkvist, V., Theorell, T., Jonsson, H., Schulman, S., Berntorp, E., & Stiegendal L. (1994). Psychosocial self prognosis in relation to mortality and morbidity in hemophiliacs with HIV infection. *Psychotherapy Psychosomatic, 62,* 185–192.

Bryk, A. S., & Raudenbush, S. W. (2002). *Hierarchical linear models: Applications and data analysis methods* (2nd ed.). Thousand Oaks, CA: Sage.

Carver, C., & Scheier, M. (1998). *On the self-regulation of behavior.* Cambridge, England: Cambridge University Press.

Carver, C. S., Scheier, M. F., & Weintraub, J. K. (1989). Assessing coping strategies: A theoretically based approach. *Journal of Personality and Social Psychology, 56,* 267–283.

Carver, C. S., Pozo, C., Harris, S. D., Noriega, B., Scheier, M. F., Robinson, D. S., Ketcham, A. S., Moffat, F. L., & Clark, K. C. (1993). How coping mediates the effect of optimism on distress: A study of women with early stage breast cancer. *Journal of Personality and Social Psychology, 65,* 375–390.

Chesney, M. A., Darbes, L. A., Hoerster, K., Taylor, J. M., Chambers, D. B., & Anderson, D. E. (2005) Positive emotions: Ex-

ploring the other hemisphere in behavioral medicine. *International Journal of Behavioral Medicine, 12*(2), 50–58.

Chesney, M. A., Ickovics, J. R., Chambers, D. B., Gifford A. L., Neidig, J., Zwickl, B., & Wu, A. W. (2000). Self-reported adherence to antiretroviral medications among participants in HIV clinical trails: The AACTG adherence instruments. Patient Care Committee and Adherence Working Group of the Outcomes Committee of the Adult AIDS Clinical Trials Group (AACTG). *AIDS Care, 12,* 255–266.

Cohen, F., Kearney, K. A., Zegans, L. S., Kemeney, M. E., Neuhaus, J. M., & Stites, D. P. (1999). Differential immune system changes with acute and persistent stress for optimists vs. pessimists. *Brain, Behavior, and Immunity, 13,* 155–174.

Cohen, L., Moor, C. de, & Amato, R. J. (2001). The association between treatment-specific optimism and depressive symptomatology in patients enrolled in a phase I cancer clinical trial. *Cancer, 91,* 1949–1955.

Cohen, S., & Williamson, G. M. (1988). Perceived stress in a probability sample of the United States. In S. Spacapan & S. Oskamp (Eds.), *The social psychology of health* (pp. 31–67). Newbury Park, CA: Sage.

Cruess, S., Antoni, M., Kilbourn, K., Ironson, G., Klimas, N., Fletcher, M. A., Baum, A., & Schneiderman, N. (2000). Optimism, distress, and immunologic status in HIV-Infected gay men following hurricane Andrew. *International Journal of Behavioral Medicine, 7,* 160–182.

Fletcher, M. A., Maher, K., Patarca, R., & Klimas, N. (2000). Comparative analysis of lymphocytes in lymph nodes and peripheral blood of patients with chronic fatigue syndrome. *Journal of the Chronic Fatigue Syndrome, 7,* 65–75.

Giltay, E. J., Geleijnse, J. M., Zitman, F. G., Hoeskstra, T., & Evert, G. S. (2004). Dispositional optimism and all-cause and cardiovascular mortality in a prospective cohort of elderly dutch men and women. *Archives of General Psychiatry, 61,* 1065–1176.

Helgeson, V. S., & Fritz, H. L. (1999). Cognitive adaptation as a predictor of new coronary events after percutaneous transluminal coronary angioplasty. *Psychosomatic Medicine, 61,* 488–495.

Helton, W. S., Dember, W. N., Warm, J. S., & Matthews, G. (2000). Optimism, pessimism, and false failure feedback: Effects of vigilance and performance. *Current Psychology: Developmental, Learning, Personality, Social, 18,* 311–325.

Holmes, W. C., & Pace, J. L. (2002). HIV-seropositive individuals' optimistic beliefs about prognosis and relation to medication and safe sex adherence. *Journal of General Internal Medicine, 17,* 677–683.

Ickovics, J. R., Hamburger, M. E., Vlahov, D., Schoenbaum, E. E., Schuman, P., Boland, R. J., Moore, J., & Vlahov, D. (2001). Mortality, CD4 cell count decline, and depressive symptoms among HIV-seropositive women: Longitudinal analysis from the HIV Epidemiology Research Study. *Journal of the American Medical Association, 285,* 1460–1465.

Ironson, G., Friedman, A., Klimas, N., Antoni M., Fletcher M. A., LaPerriere A., Simoneau J., & Schneiderman, N. (1994). Distress, denial, and low adherence to behavioral interventions predict faster disease progression in gay men infected with human immunodeficiency virus. *International Journal of Behavioral Medicine, 1,* 90–105.

Ironson, G., O'Cleirigh, C., Fletcher, M. A., Laurenceau, J. P., Balbin, E., Klimas, N., Schneiderman, N., & Solomon, G. (2005). *Psychosocial factors predict CD4 and viral load change in men and women with HIV in the era of highly active antiretroviral treatment.* Manuscript submitted for publication.

Kiecolt-Glaser, J. K., & Glaser, R. (1988). Methodological issues in behavioral immunology research with humans. *Brain, Behavior, and Immunity, 2,* 67–78.

Leserman, J. (2003). HIV disease progression: Depression, stress, and possible mechanisms. *Biological Psychiatry, 54* (3), 295–306.

Leserman, J., Petitto, J. M., Golden, R. N., Gaynes, B. N., Gu, H., Perkins, D. O., Silva, S. G., Folds, J. D., & Evans, D. L. (2000). Impact of stressful life events, depression, social support, coping and cortisol on progression to AIDS. *American Journal of Psychiatry, 157,* 1221–1228.

Milam, J. E., Richardson, J. L., Marks, G., Kemper C. A., & McCutchan A. J. (2004). The roles of dispositional optimism and pessimism in HIV disease progression. *Psychology and Health, 19,* 167–181.

Mulkana, S. S., & Hailey, B. J. (2001). The role of optimism in health-enhancing behavior. *American Journal of Health Behavior, 25,* 388–395.

Peterson, C., & Seligman, M. E. P. (1984). Causal explanations as a risk factor for depression: Theory and evidence. *Psychological Review, 91,* 347–374.

Peterson, C., & Seligman, M. E. P. (1987). Explanatory style and illness. *Journal of Personality, 55,* 237–265.

Peterson, C., Seligman, M. E. P., & Vaillant, G. (1988). Pessimistic explanatory style is a risk factor for physical illness: A thirty-five-year longitudinal study. *Journal of Personality and Social Psychology, 55,* 23–27.

Peterson, C., & Vaidya, R. S. (2003). Optimism as virtue and vice. In E. Chang & S. Lawrence (Eds.), *Virtue, vice, personality: The complexity of behavior* (pp. 23–37). Washington, DC: American Psychological Association.

Preacher, K. J., & Leonardelli, G. J. (2003). *Calculation for the Sobel Test: An interactive calculation tool for mediation tests.* Retrieved April 21, 2004 from University of North Carolina Chapel Hill Web site: http://www.unc.edu/~preacher/sobel.htm

Reed, G., Kemeny, M. E., Taylor S. E., & Visscher, B. R. (1999). Negative HIV-specific expectancies and AIDS-related bereavement as predictors of symptom onset in asymptomatic HIV-positive gay men. *Health Psychology, 18,* 354–363.

Reed, G. M., Kemeny, M. E., Taylor, S. E., Wang, H. Y. I., & Visscher, B. R. (1994). Realistic acceptance as a predictor of decreased survival time in gay men with AIDS. *Health Psychology, 13,* 299–307.

Scheier, M. F., & Carver, C. S. (1985). Optimism, coping, and health: Assessment and implications of generalized outcome expectancies. *Health Psychology, 4,* 219–247.

Scheier, M. F., & Carver, C. S. (1987). Dispositional optimism and physical well-being: The influence of generalized outcome expectancies on health. *Journal of Personality and Social Psychology, 55,* 169–210.

Scheier, M. F., Carver, C. S., & Bridges, M. W. (1994). Distinguishing optimism from neuroticism (and trait anxiety, self-mastery, and self-esteem): A re-evaluation of the Life Orientation Test. *Journal of Personality and Social Psychology, 67,* 1063–1078.

Scheier, M. F., Matthews, K., Owens, J. F., Magovern G. J., Lefebvre, R. C., Abbott, R. A., & Carver, C. S. (1989). Dispositional optimism and recovery from coronary artery bypass surgery: The beneficial effects on physical and psychological well-being. *Journal of Personality Social Psychology, 57,* 1024–1040.

Scheier, M. F., Matthews, K., Owens, J. F., Schulz, R., Bridges, M. W., Magovern, G. J., & Carver, C. S. (1999). Optimism and rehospitalization after coronary artery bypass graft surgery. *Archives of Internal Medicine, 159,* 829–835.

Schofield, P., Ball, D., Smith, J. G., Borland, R., O'Brien, P., Davis, S., Olver, I., Ryan, G., & Joseph, D. (2004). Optimism and survival in lung carcinoma patients. *Cancer, 100* (6), 1276–1282.

Schou, I., Ekeberg, Ø., Ruland, C. M., Sandvik, L., & Karesen, R. (2004). Pessimism as a predictor of emotional morbidity one year following breast cancer surgery. *Psycho-oncology, 13,* 309–320.

Schulman, P., Keith, D., & Seligman, M. E. (1993). Is optimism heritable? A study of twins. *Behaviour, Research and Therapy, 31,* 569–574.

Schulz, R., Bookwala, J., Knapp, J. E., Scheier, M., & Williamson, G. M. (1996). Pessimism, age, and cancer mortality. *Psychology and Aging, 11,* 304–309.

Segerstrom, S. C. (2001). Optimism and attentional bias for negative and positive stimuli. *Journal of Behavioral Medicine, 24* (5), 441–467.

Segerstrom, S. C., Castañeda, J. O., & Spencer, T. E. (2003). Optimism effects on cellular immunity: Testing the affective and persistence models. *Personality and Individual Differences, 35,* 1615–1624.

Segerstrom, S. C., Taylor, S. E., Kemeny, M. E., & Fahey, J. L. (1998). Optimism is associated with mood, coping, and immune change in response to stress. *Journal of Personality and Social Psychology, 74,* 1646–1655.

Seligman, M. (1991). *Learned optimism.* New York: Knopf.

Sieber, W. J., Rodin, J., Larson, L., Ortega, S., Cummings, N., Levy, S., Whiteside, T., & Herberman, R. (1992). Modulation of human natural killer cell activity by exposure to uncontrollable stress. *Brain, Behavior, and Immunity, 6,* 141–156.

Smith, T. W., Pope, M. K., Rhodewalt, F., & Poulton, J. L. (1989). Optimism, neuroticism, coping, and symptom reports: An alternative interpretation of the Life Orientation Test. *Journal of Personality and Social Psychology, 56*(4), 640–648.

Sobel, M. E. (1982). Asymptotic intervals for indirect effects in structural equations models. In S. Leinhart (Ed.), *Sociological methodology 1982* (pp. 290–312). San Francisco: Jossey-Bass.

Taylor, S. E., Kemeny, M. E., Aspinwall, L. G., Schneider, S. G., Rodriguez, R., & Herbert, M. (1992). Optimism, coping, psychological distress, and high-risk sexual behavior among men at risk for acquired immunodeficiency syndrome (AIDS). *Journal of Personality and Social Psychology, 63,* 460–473.

Taylor, S. E., Kemeny, M. E., Bower, J. E., Gruenewald, T. L., & Reed, M. G. (2000). Psychological resources, positive illusions, and health. *American Psychologist, 55,* 99–109.

Tomakowsky, J., Lumley, M. A., Markowitz, N., & Frank, C. (2001). Optimism explanatory style and dispositional optimism in HIV-infected men. *Journal of Psychosomatic Research, 51,* 577–587.

Vos, T., Haby, M. M., Barendregt, J. J., Kruijshaar, M., Corry, J., & Andrews, G. (2004). The burden of major depression avoidable by longer-term strategies. *Archives of General Psychiatry, 61,* 1097–1103.

International Journal of Behavioral Medicine
2005, Vol. 12, No. 2, 98–102

Sense of Coherence and Biomarkers of Health in 43-Year-Old Women

Petra Lindfors, Olle Lundberg, and Ulf Lundberg

The aim of this cross-sectional study was to investigate how sense of coherence (SOC) relates to biomarkers of health in 43-year-old nonsmoking premenopausal women. Before taking part in a standardized medical health examination including assessment of blood pressure, blood lipids, and physical symptoms, participants completed a three-item measure of SOC. On the basis of their SOC scores, the 244 women with complete datasets were categorized into 1 of 3 groups with a weak, intermediate, or strong SOC. Results showed that women with a strong SOC had significantly lower levels of systolic blood pressure (p < .05) and total cholesterol (p < .05) than did women with a weak SOC. It is suggested that the lower levels of systolic blood pressure and total cholesterol found in women with a strong SOC may constitute a biological buffer against ill health and disease.

Key words: sense of coherence, blood pressure, blood lipids, medical examination, women

According to Antonovsky's (1987) salutogenic approach, an individual's sense of coherence (SOC) is crucial to long-term health and well-being. The SOC concept consists of three theoretically related dimensions of comprehensibility, manageability, and meaningfulness. Together these dimensions depict a global orientation. Antonovsky (1987) defines this global orientation as the extent to which an individual perceives and interprets stimuli from different aspects of the environment as structured, predictable, and understandable. The global orientation also involves the individual's taking into consideration whether there are resources available for dealing with the demands posed from the stimuli and whether these demands are challenging and need to be dealt with. The fundamental assumption of the conceptualization of SOC is that daily life is complex and involves being confronted with various stimuli. These stimuli can be more or less contradictory and dealing with them may lead to tension and stress. Antonovsky (1987, 1993a) argues that this type of tension and stress has to be resolved to avoid negative stress. To deal successfully with everyday stimuli and remain healthy, all three parts of SOC are needed: An individual has to know how to deal with something and be able to do that and grasp the meaning of the actions taken.

Following Antonovsky (1987), individuals with a strong SOC are considered to view life as sufficiently structured to allow a certain degree of predictability and intelligibility of events coupled with a belief in having access to necessary resources for handling various demands. In contrast, individuals with a weak SOC view life as unorganized and meaningless and are lacking in resources to deal with daily life. Consequently, individuals with a strong SOC are more likely to stay healthy compared to individuals with a weak SOC, particularly during times of adversity (Antonovsky, 1987, 1993a; see also Surtees, Wainwright, Luben, Khaw, & Day, 2003).

There are several versions of self-report inventories available for the measurement of SOC, including a 29-item version (Antonovsky, 1987) and an easily administered three-item version (Lundberg & Nyström Peck, 1995). Factorial and structural analyses of these measures have shown that the different dimensions of SOC are strongly interrelated, which supports the proposed unidimensionality of the SOC concept (Antonovsky, 1987; Feldt, Leskinen, Kinnunen, & Mauno, 2000; Feldt & Rasku, 1998). Although findings indicating close negative relations between SOC and nega-

Petra Lindfors and Ulf Lundberg at the Centre for Health Equity Studies (CHESS) and the Department of Psychology, Stockholm University, Stockholm, Sweden; Olle Lundberg, the Centre for Health Equity Studies (CHESS), Stockholm University, Stockholm, Sweden.

We are grateful to the women who volunteered to participate in this study that was part of the longitudinal research program Individual Development and Adaptation led by Professor Lars R. Bergman at the Department of Psychology, Stockholm University. Further thanks to the IDA II research team and to Ola Andersson for managing the data. Financial support for the data collection came from the Swedish Committee for the Planning and Coordination of Research, the Swedish Social Science Research Council, and the Örebro City Council. This study was supported by grants to Professor Ulf Lundberg from the Bank of Sweden Tercentenary Foundation and the Swedish Research Council.

Correspondence concerning this article should be addressed to Petra Lindfors, Centre for Health Equity Studies (CHESS), Stockholm University, S–106 91 Stockholm, Sweden. E-mail: pls@psychology.su.se

tive affectivity or depression have raised doubts as to whether SOC mainly reflects the absence of neuroticism (Geyer, 1997; Kravetz, Drory, & Florina, 1993), other studies have demonstrated the solid criterion validity of the SOC measure (Antonovsky, 1987, 1993b; Feldt & Rasku, 1998; Pallant & Lae, 2002; Smith & Meyer, 1997). Furthermore, a number of studies have supported Antonovsky's (1987) theory in demonstrating that SOC is negatively related to various types of ill health and disease including physical symptoms (e.g., Lundberg & Nyström Peck, 1994; Runeson, Norbäck, & Stattin, 2003), poor lipid profiles (Svartvik et al., 2000), and coronary heart disease (e.g., Poppius, Tenkanen, Kalimo, & Heinsalmi, 1999) and positively related to subjective health status (e.g., Suominen, Helenius, Blomberg, Uutela, & Koskenvuo, 2001) and reduced risks for all-cause mortality (Surtees et al., 2003).

Although several studies have described how SOC is associated with various health-related outcomes including disease and mortality, there have been few attempts to characterize the physiological mechanisms underlying these relations in healthy individuals representative of the general population. In keeping with Antonovsky's (1987) line of reasoning, an individual's SOC may modify a stress reaction in different ways at different stages of the process. For instance, an individual with a strong SOC does not evaluate stimuli as stressful and consequently does not experience the subsequent tension and stress that is experienced by individuals with a weak SOC. Considering that the health-related outcomes of a strong and weak SOC are distinct (e.g., Antonovsky, 1987), these differences ought to be discernible in the physiological processes preceding various types of diseases (i.e., risk factors). Accordingly, individuals with distinct profiles of SOC would be expected to have different health profiles not only in terms of symptoms and diseases but also in terms of biomarkers for health or risk factors for disease.

Among the easily assessed and reliable biomarkers providing estimates of the health status of different bodily systems are those that may be obtained through standardized medical examinations, which include assessment of physical symptoms as well as cardiovascular measures and lipid profiles. So far, this approach has only been used with the 29-item version of the SOC measure in one screening study of cardiovascular risk in postmenopausal women (Svartvik et al., 2000). In addition to an inverse association between SOC and symptoms, Svartvik et al. (2000) found that women reporting a weak SOC had poorer lipid profiles, characterized by low levels of high-density lipoproteins (HDLs) and high levels of triglycerides, than did women with a stronger SOC. Increasing levels of these biomarkers, such as higher blood pressure, higher levels of total cholesterol, and lower levels of HDLs, have

repeatedly been associated with acute and long-term stress and subsequent disease (Hjemdahl, 2000; McCann et al., 1999; Stoney & Finney, 2000). In contrast, lower and stable levels within an optimal range have been considered to reflect health.

The objective of the present cross-sectional study was to investigate how SOC, as assessed with the aforementioned three-item measure, relates to physiological indicators including cardiovascular and lipid measures as well as ratings of physical symptoms obtained from standardized medical examinations of 43-year-old nonsmoking women of a cohort representative of the general population. Drawing on previous studies (e.g., Lundberg & Nyström Peck, 1994; Svartvik et al., 2000), women with a strong SOC were hypothesized to have better health status showing optimal cardiovascular and lipid profiles and reporting fewer symptoms than women with a weak SOC.

Method

Participants

Data came from the 1998 data collection within the Individual Development and Adaptation research program (Bergman, 2000; Magnusson, 1988) that includes individuals living in Örebro, a middle-sized Swedish town. Questionnaires were administered to all of the then 43-year-old women ($N = 569$) participating in the study, and a smaller but representative subsample was asked to participate in a routine medical examination. Of the 369 women who took part in the medical examination, complete data from both the health checkup and questionnaires were made available for 337 participants. However, because smoking and menopause are known have effects on blood pressure and blood lipids, the statistical analyses included the 244 nonsmoking premenopausal women only. The study was approved by a local ethics committee.

Medical Examination

All medical examinations were performed by a district nurse at a local county health care center. The examination involved the measurement of height, weight, blood pressure, heart rate (HR), and blood sampling. In addition to these tests, a subsequent health checkup was performed by either of two local general practitioners (both women). The procedure was analogous to those regularly performed at the community health care centers and, thus, was highly representative for examinations in general practice. Weight and height, used in calculating body mass index (BMI; kg/m^2), were measured without shoes in very lightweight indoor clothing. Weight was measured to 0.1-kg accuracy using a digital scale: Lindeltronic 4000 (Lindells,

Malmö, Sweden). Waist circumference (cm) was measured at the spina iliaca anterior superior and hip circumference (cm) at the trochanter major and then was used to calculate waist-to-hip ratio (WHR). A TriCuff® and HELP® heart level pillow (AJ Medical, Lidingö, Sweden) were used to assess systolic blood pressure (SBP; mm Hg), diastolic blood pressure (DBP; mm Hg), and HR (beats/min) twice after 5 min of rest. Blood samples were drawn in fasting state to determine blood glucose and blood lipids, including total cholesterol and HDL. Due to differences in routine analysis of blood lipids, triglycerides were available for approximately one fifth of the participants and additional information concerning levels of circulating low-density lipoproteins (LDLs) was calculated for this group using Friedewald's formula. Symptoms were rated by the local general practitioner following a list of 12 conditions including asthma, birthmarks, breast problems, heart problems, lung problems, lymph gland problems, mouth and throat problems, musculoskeletal problems, stomach problems, tender points, and thyroid problems. Current health problems were rated as (0) and the absence of health problems was rated as (1). For the statistical analysis, ratings across the different symptoms were added to create a composite index of physical symptoms with scores ranging from 0 to 12 with high scores indicating fewer symptoms and better physician-rated health. Nicotine consumption (i.e., smoking and using snuff) was assessed using single-item questions with dichotomous response alternatives (yes/no). Finally, all women were asked questions on the time and regularity of periods and whether they received hormone replacement therapy or experienced any kind of menopausal symptoms such as irregular periods or hot flushes.

Questionnaire

Participants answered the three-item version of SOC that has been evaluated in a representative sample of the Swedish population aged 25–75 years (Lundberg & Nyström Peck, 1995). Based on the theoretical reasoning underlying Antonovsky's (1987) original instrument, this measure consists of three questions, each corresponding to one of the dimensions (i.e., manageability, meaningfulness, and comprehensibility) covered by the original instrument: (a) Do you usually see solutions to problems and difficulties that other people find hopeless? (manageability), (b) Do you usually feel that your daily life is a source of personal satisfaction? (meaningfulness), and (c) Do you usually feel that the things that happen to you in your daily life are hard to understand? (comprehensibility). Answers are indicated within a 3-point response format including 0 *(yes, usually)*, 1 *(yes sometimes)*, and 2 *(no)*. After reversing the scores on the third question, an additive index was calculated with high scores indicating a weak SOC. Previously established cutoff values where scores above 3 indicate a weak SOC, 1 to 2 an intermediate SOC, and 0 a strong SOC (Lundberg & Nyström Peck, 1994, 1995) were used to obtain groups of individuals with distinct profiles of SOC. Previous studies of the three-item measure have shown satisfactory test–retest reliability ($\kappa = .61$) and factor analyses have shown that the items constitute a single factor similar to that of the original SOC measure (Lundberg & Nyström Peck, 1994, 1995). There is also a strong relation ($r = .66$) between the three-item measure and the original scale. Moreover, the relations between the three-item measure and other variables have been found to be similar to those found in research using the original 29-item SOC measure (Lundberg & Nyström Peck, 1994; Surtees et al., 2003).

Statistical Analysis

Having divided the sample into three groups with a weak, intermediate, and a strong SOC and concluding that all individuals were nonsmoking premenopausal women, means and standard deviations for all the physiological indicators were calculated for each group. Differences between groups were analyzed using one-way analysis of variance (ANOVA). Significant differences were further examined by post hoc comparisons using the Bonferroni method.

Results

Scores on the SOC measure ranged from 0 to 5 with an arithmetic mean of 1.5 ($SD = 1.1$) and a median of 1.0. As shown in Table 1, categorization of the participants using established cutoff values revealed that 59.4% ($n = 145$) of the women had an intermediate SOC, whereas 22.1 % ($n = 54$) had a strong SOC, and 18.5% ($n = 45$) a weak SOC.

Physiological profiles of women with a weak, intermediate, and strong SOC are presented in Table 1. For ratings of physical symptoms made by the general practitioners, there were no significant differences between the groups, $F(2, 241) = .99$, p not significant (ns). Considering cardiovascular measures, there were significant differences in SBP, $F(2, 241) = 4.34$, $p < .05$, between women with different profiles of SOC. Post hoc comparisons showed that women with a strong SOC had significantly lower SBP than did women with a weak SOC ($p < .05$). For DBP, the differences in mean values followed the same pattern but failed to reach statistical significance, $F(2, 241) = 2.32$, p ns. With respect to HR, no significant differences were found, $F(2, 241) = .90$, p ns. Further analyses showed no significant differences in BMI, $F(2,$

Table 1. *Physiological Profiles as Related to Weak, Intermediate, and Strong SOC in 43-Year-Old Women*

	Sense of Coherence					
	Weak (n = 45) 18.5%		Intermediate (n = 145) 59.4%		Strong (n = 54) 22.1%	
Biomarker	M	SD	M	SD	M	SD
Physical symptoms	9.8	1.3	9.9	1.1	10.0	0.9
SBP[a]	129.4	18.7	124.2	15.6	119.9	14.8
DBP	77.5	12.9	75.5	9.9	73.1	8.5
HR	70.7	9.8	70.5	9.8	68.6	8.6
BMI	26.0	4.2	24.8	4.1	24.3	4.2
WHR	.95	0.04	.95	0.04	.94	0.04
Glucose	4.3	1.1	4.5	1.2	4.3	1.6
Total cholesterol[a]	5.6	0.9	5.3	0.9	5.1	1.0
HDL	1.7	0.5	1.8	0.4	1.8	0.4
	Weak (n = 9) 16.4%		Intermediate (n = 37) 67.3%		Strong (n = 9) 16.4%	
LDL	3.3	1.3	2.9	0.9	3.0	0.8
LDL/HDL	2.2	1.3	1.7	0.8	1.9	0.7
Triglycerides	1.5	1.1	1.1	0.4	1.0	0.5

Notes. BMI = body mass index; DBP = diastolic blood pressure; HDL = high-density lipoprotein; HR = heart rate; LDL = low-density lipoprotein; SBP = systolic blood pressure; SOC = sense of coherence; WHR = waist-to-hip ratio.
[a]Post hoc tests show significant differences between groups with weak and strong SOC ($p < .05$).

241) $= 2.38$, p ns; WHR, $F(2, 241) = 1.84$, p ns; or blood glucose levels, $F(2, 241) = .38$, p ns, between the groups. For blood lipids, significant differences emerged for total cholesterol, $F(2, 241) = 4.35$, $p < .05$. Subsequent post hoc comparisons showed that women with a strong SOC had significantly lower levels of total cholesterol than did women with a weak SOC ($p < .05$). However, there were no significant differences in HDL, $F(2, 241) = 1.98$, p ns. The levels of LDL, $F(2, 52) = .58$, p ns; LDL/HDL, $F(2, 52) = .80$, p ns; and triglycerides, $F(2, 52) = 2.50$, p ns, seemed higher in women with a weak SOC but these group differences did not reach statistical significance in the small subsample.

Discussion

Using the easily administered three-item measure of SOC, this study showed significant differences in SBP and total cholesterol within the normal range in otherwise healthy 43-year-old nonsmoking premenopausal women with distinct profiles of SOC. More specifically, women with a strong SOC had significantly lower SBP and lower levels of circulating total cholesterol than did women with a weak SOC. As for cardiovascular measures, significant differences relating to SOC were found for SBP only. However, a similar pattern was found for DBP (Table 1). These findings are largely in line with the initial hypotheses, and the results concerning blood lipids to some extent

replicate findings from a previous study (Svartvik et al., 2000). However, although Svartvik et al. (2000) found that a weak SOC was related to low levels of HDL, our research showed relations with high total cholesterol. The lipid profiles indicated higher levels of LDL, LDL/HDL, and triglycerides in women with a weak SOC (Table 1) but none of these differences reached statistical significance for this small group ($n = 9$). In contrast to previous findings, our study showed no significant differences in physical symptoms in women with different profiles of SOC. The slight differences in the research findings concerning lipid profiles and symptoms are most probably due to age differences between the samples that influence the physiological parameters (McEwen, 1998; Stoney & Finney, 2000) and to variations in the methods used in assessing symptoms.

Looking at the results from this study, the physiological profiles of women with a stronger SOC indicate that their cardiovascular and lipid systems are less exhausted than those of women with a weak SOC. From this it can be hypothesized first that, in their attempt to handle daily life, women with a strong SOC experience less stress than women with a weak SOC and, second, that the cumulative effects of the higher stress in the latter group manifest themselves in poorer physiological profiles. Although this may result in cardiovascular disease in women with a weak SOC, those with a strong SOC stay healthy because their physiological systems are protected from the wear and tear of daily stress.

In considering the potential impact of psychosocial factors on these findings, the differences in biomarkers found here may also result from the fact that SOC is strongly associated with other psychosocial factors, such as self-esteem, adaptive coping, depression, and hostility. These psychosocial factors may have acted as confounders because they are already known to influence health. However, in a recent study on women, a weak SOC, but not depression, was found to drive the negative effects of hostility on health (Kivimäki et al., 2002). Moreover, the relation between a strong SOC and reduced mortality, reported by Surtees et al. (2003), was not associated with other psychosocial factors.

Looking at other possible explanations of the results, the lower blood pressure and lower levels of total cholesterol found in women with a strong SOC may be related not only to control and personal resources but also to lifestyle factors such as dietary intake and regular physical exercise. In considering the potential influence of such lifestyle factors on physiological indicators, both dietary habits and physical exercise may influence WHR, BMI, or glucose. However, there were no significant differences in these physiological indicators between the groups studied here.

Obviously, the conclusions from this research are limited by the cross-sectional design, the sample characteristics and the lack of background information on socioeconomic position, family situation, work stress, and other psychosocial factors that might affect both SOC and physiological indicators. However, in including healthy nonsmoking middle-aged premenopausal women representative for this group of the general population, the study clarifies the physiological processes associated with different profiles of SOC. Moreover, in yielding results similar to research using the original version of SOC, this study, using a more easily administered three-item SOC scale, suggests that SOC is manifested in physiological processes. This finding opens up a biological pathway to health and well-being.

References

Antonovsky, A. (1987). *Unraveling the mystery of health.* San Francisco: Jossey-Bass.

Antonovsky, A. (1993a). Complexity, conflict, chaos, coherence, coercion and civility. *Social Science and Medicine, 37,* 969–981.

Antonovsky, A. (1993b). The structure and properties of the sense of coherence scale. *Social Science and Medicine, 36,* 725–733.

Bergman, L. R. (2000). *Women's health, work, and education in a life-span perspective. Technical report 1: Theoretical background and overview of the data collection* (Report from the project Individual Development and Adaptation No. 70.). Stockholm, Sweden: Stockholm University, Department of Psychology.

Feldt, T., Leskinen, E., Kinnunen, U., & Mauno, S. (2000). Longitudinal factor analysis models in the assessment of the stability of sense of coherence. *Personality and Individual Differences, 28,* 239–257.

Feldt, T., & Rasku, A. (1998). The structure of Antonovsky's orientation to life questionnaire. *Personality and Individual Differences, 25,* 505–516.

Geyer, S. (1997). Some conceptual considerations on the sense of coherence. *Social Science and Medicine, 44,* 1771–1779.

Hjemdahl, P. (2000). Cardiovascular system and stress. In G. Fink (Ed.), *Encyclopedia of stress* (Vol. 1, pp. 389–403). San Diego, CA: Academic.

Kivimäki, M., Elovainio, M., Vahtera, J., Nurmi, J. E., Feldt, T., Keltikangas-Järvinen, L., & Pentti, J. (2002). Sense of coherence as a mediator between hostility and health. Seven-year prospective study on female employees. *Journal of Psychosomatic Research, 52,* 239–247.

Kravetz, S., Drory, Y., & Florina, V. (1993). Hardiness and sense of coherence and their relation to negative affect. *European Journal of Personality, 7,* 233–244.

Lundberg, O., & Nyström Peck, M. (1994). Sense of coherence, social structure and health. Evidence from a population survey in Sweden. *European Journal of Public Health, 4,* 252–257.

Lundberg, O., & Nyström Peck, M. (1995). A simplified way of measuring sense of coherence. *European Journal of Public Health, 5,* 56–59.

Magnusson, D. (1988). *Individual development from an interactional perspective: A longitudinal study.* Hillsdale, NJ: Lawrence Erlbaum Associates, Inc.

McCann, B. S., Benjamin, G. A., Wilkinson, C. W., Retzlaff, B. M., Russo, J., & Knopp, R. H. (1999). Plasma lipid concentrations during occupational stress. *Annals of Behavioral Medicine, 21,* 103–110.

McEwen, B. S. (1998). Protective and damaging effects of stress mediators: Allostasis and allostatic load. *New England Journal of Medicine, 338,* 171–179.

Pallant, J. F., & Lae, L. (2002). Sense of coherence, well-being, coping, and personality factors: Further evaluation of the sense of coherence scale. *Personality and Individual Differences, 33,* 39–48.

Poppius, E., Tenkanen, L., Kalimo, R., & Heinsalmi, P. (1999). The sense of coherence, occupation and the risk of coronary heart disease in the Helsinki Heart Study. *Social Science and Medicine, 49,* 109–120.

Runeson, R., Norbäck, D., & Stattin, H. (2003). Symptoms and sense of coherence—a follow-up study of personnel from workplace buildings with indoor air problems. *International Archives of Occupational and Environmental Health, 76,* 29–38.

Smith, T. L., & Meyer, L. S. (1997). The sense of coherence: Its relationship to personality, stress, and health measures. *Journal of Social Behavior and Personality, 12,* 513–527.

Stoney, C. M., & Finney, M. (2000). Cholesterol and lipoproteins. In G. Fink (Ed.), *Encyclopedia of stress* (Vol. 1, pp. 454–459). San Diego, CA: Academic.

Suominen, S., Helenius, H., Blomberg, H., Uutela, A., & Koskenvuo M. (2001). Sense of coherence as a predictor of subjective state of health: Results from 4 years of follow-up of adults. *Journal of Psychosomatic Research, 50,* 77–86.

Surtees, P., Wainwright, N., Luben, R., Khaw, K-T., & Day, N. (2003). Sense of coherence and mortality in men and women in the EPIC-Norfolk United Kingdom prospective Cohort Study. *American Journal of Epidemiology, 158,* 1202–1209.

Svartvik, L., Lidfeldt, J., Nerbrand, C., Samsiö, G., Scherstén, B., & Nilsson, P. M. (2000). Dyslipidaemia and impaired well-being in middle-aged women reporting low sense of coherence. *Scandinavian Journal of Primary Health Care, 18,* 177–182.

International Journal of Behavioral Medicine
2005, Vol. 12, No. 2, 103–110

Relations Between Companion Animals and Self-Reported Health in Older Women: Cause, Effect or Artifact?

Nancy A. Pachana, Jessica H. Ford, Brooke Andrew, and Annette J. Dobson

A large longitudinal dataset on women's health in Australia provided the basis of analysis of potential positive health effects of living with a companion animal. Age, living arrangements, and housing all strongly related to both living with companion animals and health. Methodological problems in using data from observational studies to disentangle a potential association in the presence of substantial effects of demographic characteristics are highlighted. Our findings may help to explain some inconsistencies and contradictions in the literature about the health benefits of companion animals, as well as offer suggestions for ways to move forward in future investigations of human–pet relationships.

Key words: companion animals; women's health; epidemiology; methodology; sociodemographics

Animals are such agreeable friends—they ask no questions, they pass no criticisms.

George Eliot, *Scenes from Clerical Life* (1857)

Characteristics of Pet Owners

The literature examining relations between ownership of companion animals and health and well-being is inconsistent. The relationships between participants and their pets, measures used to determine health and well-being, analyses used, and conclusions drawn all vary widely. The types of studies reported range from anecdotal case reports and small observational studies to large-scale epidemiological studies. Although much of the descriptive literature tends to support the benefits of animal companionship, large-scale analytic studies yield inconsistent and even contradictory findings.

The literature has been most informative and least controversial on the issue of the demographic and social context variables associated with ownership of companion animals. For example, data from a number of sources characterize pet owners as younger and more likely to be married and living with children than non–pet owners (American Veterinary Medical Association, 1993; McHarg, Baldock, Headey, & Robinson, 1995). Studies conducted with older adults (aged about 60 years and older) show a similar pattern (Lawton,

Moss, & Moles, 1984; Raina, Walter-Toews, Bonnett, Woodward, & Abernathy, 1999; Simons, Simons, McCallum, & Friedlander, 2000). Pet owners are also more likely to reside in unattached houses than any other type of dwelling (Lawton et al., 1984; Netting, Wilson, & Fruge, 1988; Raina et al., 1999; Wells & Rodi, 2000), with the size of the yard associated with the dwelling another important factor in determining pet ownership (McHarg et al., 1995). Gender also influences pet ownership, with women and those with a more sedentary lifestyle more likely to own cats than dogs (Friedmann & Thomas, 1995; Serpell, 1991). Finally, although several studies report no differences in socioeconomic status (SES) between pet owners and non–pet owners (McHarg et al., 1995; Raina et al., 1999; Simons, McCallum, & Simons, 1997), Parslow and Jorm (2003), using education as a marker of SES, found that pet owners had less education than non–pet owners. In addition, surveys of older people suggest that having a lower income is a contributing factor to nonownership of pets (Lawton et al., 1984; Wilson & Netting, 1987).

The benefits reported from companion animals are generally consistent with the benefits identified through research into social support and attachment and suggest that human–pet companionship may promote health and positive well-being in ways similar to human–human interactions (Garrity & Stallones, 1998; Garrity, Stallones, Marx, & Johnson, 1989; Ory & Goldberg, 1983). Human–pet interactions, like human social relationships, may contribute to emotional and social well-being (Sable, 1995). The provision of emotional support by pets across a range of groups, including children, adolescents, single women, and the elderly, has been demonstrated in many studies

Nancy A. Pachana and Brooke Andrew at the School of Psychology, University of Queensland, Brisbane, Queensland, Australia; Jessica H. Ford and Annette J. Dobson at the School of Population Health, University of Queensland, Brisbane, Queensland, Australia.

Correspondence concerning this article should be addressed to Nancy A. Pachana, School of Psychology, University of Queensland, Brisbane, Qld 4072, Australia. E-mail: n.pachana@psy.uq.edu.au

(Bodsworth & Coleman, 2001; Sable, 1995; Siegal, 1990; Zasloff & Kidd, 1994).

Health Benefits and Companion Animals

The results of studies examining the role of companion animals in health outcomes are varied. This literature is for the most part comprised of studies that have pet ownership as a variable, controlled to some extent but not truly "experimental" in design. A truly experimental study of pet ownership would include random assignment of companion animals, because many variables can lead individuals to either own or not own pets. Also, ideally such experimental systems should be as closed as possible, to eliminate as many sources of error variance as possible. For example, looking at individuals' responses to pictures of animals could be considered experimental in nature (Lipp, Derakshan, Waters, & Logies, 2004); exploring the difference between blood pressure when a companion animal is or is not present with their owner meets these basic criteria (Eddy, 1996). However, the latter studies, although more experimental in nature, do not have explicit health outcomes.

The common practice of reporting health benefits in groups of pet and non–pet-owning samples does not meet these criteria for experimental research, being largely correlational in nature. For example, Allen, Blascovitch, and Mendes (2002) examined pet and non–pet owner's cardiovascular reactivity in the face of a variety of stressor conditions (e.g., mental arithmetic tasks). The results largely demonstrate that pet owners' responses were different than non–pet owners, but because pet ownership was not experimentally manipulated, the results could also reflect differences in the groups rather than an effect of how pets are viewed (as social support mechanisms in stressful situations) or that pets somehow buffer stress responses more generally.

Truly experimental research on the effects of pet ownership on health outcomes is rare. An earlier study by Allen, Shykoff, and Izzo (2001) does satisfy these criteria. In this study, half of a non–pet owning sample (stockbrokers with hypertension) were randomly assigned to adopt a pet cat or dog. All were started on antihypertensive medication, which was effective in lowering blood pressure. However, the participants who had acquired an animal demonstrated smaller blood pressure increases while under stress than those participants who had not acquired a pet.

The majority of the extant literature then can best be described as observational or quasiexperimental in nature rather than being truly experimental. The studies cited later, and this study, fall into this category. If the data from such studies are interpreted with caution, and

their methodological limitations carefully considered, then potential avenues for future, possibly experimental research on these issues, such as the study by Allen et al. (2001), can be pursued.

Pet ownership has also been explored in the epidemiological literature. Simons et al. (2000) reported the results of a longitudinal study of older people as showing no significant relation between pet ownership and all-cause mortality. A lack of positive changes in physical and mental health, and psychological well-being has also been reported in another longitudinal study (Raina et al., 1999). Friedmann and coauthors (Friedmann, Katcher, Lynch, & Thomas, 1980; Friedmann & Thomas, 1995) have found pet ownership to be associated with better survival among cardiac patients, whereas other investigators (e.g., Anderson, Reid & Jennings, 1992) found pet owners had lower levels of cardiovascular risk factors. Limited support for better mental health among cat owners compared to non–cat owners was found by Straede and Gates (1993). Simple acquisition of pets has also been linked to positive outcomes (Serpell, 1991).

Results are similarly mixed when the extent of attachment to pets is examined (Parslow & Jorm, 2003; Sable, 1995; Serpell, 1991; Stallones, Marx, Garrity, & Johnson, 1991). Diversity of conceptualizations of pet attachment, atheoretical development of such measures, and little psychometric support for some pet attachment scales limits their utility. Melson (1989) among others highlights the need for more rigorous methodology in the development and use of scales to measure attachment to pets.

Pets may buffer the impact of stress, thereby improving or maintaining good health. Raina et al. (1999) suggest that pet ownership appeared to buffer the negative impact of lack of social support on psychological well-being. In a longitudinal study of stressful life events on physician utilization behavior, Siegel (1990) found that respondents who owned pets reported fewer doctor contacts over the 1-year period than non–pet owners. The positive buffering effects of pets on children suffering posttraumatic stress reactions were reported by Arambasic, Kerestes, Kuterovac-Jagodic, and Vizek-Vidovic (2000).

Pet ownership has been found to be associated with physical activity. Anderson et al. (1992) found that pet owners were significantly more likely to report taking vigorous exercise three or more times per week than non–pet owners. Similarly, Wells and Rodi (2000) reported that people who owned dogs rated themselves as being more physically active than others their age. Other large-scale studies, however, have found no significant differences in physical activity between pet owners and non–pet owners (Parslow & Jorm, 2003; Simons et al., 2000). Indeed, Bauman, Russell, Furber, and Dobson (2001) found that, in general, dog owners are not more active than nonowners unless they are part of the small minority that practice regular, sustained dog walking. In a longitudinal sample, Simons et al. (2000) found that pet ownership was not significantly related to activity of daily living (ADL) levels at follow-up, whereas a Canadian longitudinal study (Raina et al., 1999) found that pet owners reported a relatively higher ADL level than non–pet owners.

Finally, it has been suggested that the benefits of companion animals are apparent only in certain situations or circumstances (Garrity & Stallones, 1998). For example, in their study of the associations between pet ownership and aspects of psychological well-being in older women, Ory and Goldberg (1983) found that among those with high SES, pet ownership was positively associated with happiness although pet ownership was negatively related to happiness among those of lower SES. In addition, some studies have suggested that improvements in psychological well-being and social interaction associated with pet companionship may be more marked for those who live alone than for those living with others (Goldmeier, 1986; Kiel, 1998; McHarg et al., 1995). Other investigators however, have suggested that those who appear to benefit most from pets are likely to already be well supported in their social relationships (Wells & Rodi, 2000).

Confounding and Effect Modification

In most of these studies on the relation between companion animals and health, although sociodemographic characteristics are measured and discussed and the potential impact of these variables on health and well-being is noted, the impact of such variables *on pet ownership itself* are only mentioned in passing and have not been fully explored. For example, increasing age is associated with increased risk for physical morbidity and is also associated with increased risk of moving to institutional care settings. Both decreased physical health and a move to assisted care can be associated with cessation of pet ownership irrespective of the wishes of the owner and irrespective to attachment bonds. Similarly, most pet owners live with other people and it is difficult to disentangle the benefits and emotional support derived from animals and people. It is also possible that variations across studies in regard to sociodemographic variables may account for the inconsistent findings on the effects of companion animals on health.

In this article we examine both cross-sectional and longitudinal associations between pet ownership and physical and mental health while controlling for demographic characteristics and other potential modifying factors. This objective also assists in identifying methodological problems that may result in inconsistent findings in this research area.

Methods

The Australian Longitudinal Study on Women's Health (ALSWH) is a survey of the health and well-being of three cohorts of women who were aged 18–23 years (younger cohort), 45–50 years (mid-age cohort), and 70–75 years (older cohort) when recruited in 1996 and who will be followed longitudinally for 20 years. The study uses mailed questionnaires to collect self-report data on health and related variables. Each age cohort is surveyed every 3 years. The overall goal of the ALSWH is to understand factors that affect the health and well-being of women.

Women were selected from the Australian national health insurance database (Medicare), which includes almost all citizens and permanent residents. Stratified random sampling was used with intentional oversampling of women from rural and remote areas. Details of the cohorts and recruitment methods have been described elsewhere (Brown et al., 1998).

Only the older women were asked in more than one survey if they lived with pets so only this cohort is discussed in this article. However, because the effects of pets on such vulnerable population subgroups as older women have been documented in the literature, the analysis of this cohort is of value. Survey 1 was completed by a total of 12,432 women in the older cohort. Of these, 7,952 women completed both Survey 2 (1999) and Survey 3 (2002), which included questions about pets. These women were 73–78 years old at Survey 2 and 76–81 years old at Survey 3. When participants with missing data were dropped, a final sample size of 6,404 women remained. This total is the basis for subsequent analyses in this article.

Instruments

For Survey 2, women were asked: "Do you have any pets in your household?"; possible responses included no pet, dog, cat, fish, horse, bird, other. For Survey 3 women were asked the same question but with fewer possible response categories: no pet, dog, cat, bird, other. Because the focus of the ALSWH is general health outcomes rather than companion animals, a scale of attachment to pets was not used. Women were categorized into four groups at both surveys: no pet, dog, cat, and other (including birds, fish, and other animals). If more than one pet was reported, respondents were assigned to a single category in a hierarchical fashion, with the hierarchical order being no pet, dog, cat, and other (e.g., women with a dog and cat were assigned to the dog category). A small number of women also changed pet ownership categories from Survey 2 to Survey 3.

The widely used, reliable, and well-validated Medical Outcomes Study's Short Form Functioning and

Well-Being profile (SF–36) is used in the ALSWH (Ware & Sherbourne, 1992; for a comprehensive review of the scale see Ware, 1999). For these analyses the Physical Functioning (PF) and Mental Health (MHI) subscales were used as outcome measures.

Sociodemographic variables were chosen to reflect those cited in previous literature (e.g. Raina, et al., 1999), which demonstrated relations with animal companionship and which were collected in the ALSWH. Explanatory factors included in both cross-sectional and longitudinal analyses were level of physical activity, ability to manage on available income, area of residence, living arrangements, housing, and moved house in the last 3 years.

Statistical Analyses

Analyses were performed using SAS version 8.02. To examine the cross-sectional associations between companion animal status and the various sociodemographic variables, analyses were performed using the SAS procedure FREQ. The results are reported from Survey 2 only. To estimate the effects of compan-

ion animal status and various sociodemographic variables on MHI and PF, random effects models were used to analyze the data simultaneously from Surveys 2 and 3. From these models, fitted using the SAS procedure MIXED, we estimated mean effects and 95% confidence limits for MHI and PF by companion animal status at each survey, adjusted for all other factors in the model. Post hoc comparisons of pairwise differences were used to identify significant effects.

Results

Table 1 shows strong associations between living with a companion animal and household arrangements, including type of housing, area of residence, and ability to manage on their income. Companion animal status was also related to levels of physical activity, although the patterns were inconsistent. Many of these variables are also strongly related to both mental and physical health (Lee, 2001; Mishra, Ball, Dobson, Byles, & Warner-Smith, 2002). Therefore, confounding is potentially an issue with respect to pet ownership and sociodemographic variables.

Table 1. *Associations Between Living With Companion Animals and Various Sociodemographic Variables Measured at Survey 2*

| Variable and *p* value | N^a(6,404) | % total | Companion Animal Status | | | |
			No Pet(*n* = 4,094)	Dog(*n*= 1,322)	Cat(*n* = 593)	Other(*n* = 395)
Level of physical activity (*p* = .04)						
None	1,790	28.0	27.1	29.7	29.7	27.9
Low	1,951	30.5	31.4	26.9	32.7	29.1
Moderate	1,054	16.5	17.0	16.0	14.7	15.4
High	1,384	21.6	21.1	24.0	19.2	22.8
Missing	225	3.5	3.4	3.5	3.7	4.8
Moved house (*p* < .0001)						
No	5,773	90.2	88.7	91.5	95.1	92.7
Yes	631	9.8	11.3	8.5	4.9	7.3
Manage on income (*p* < .0001)						
Impossible/difficult all the time	316	4.9	4.4	7.0	3.9	5.3
Difficult some of the time	1,243	19.4	17.4	23.9	22.8	20.5
Not too bad	3,307	51.6	52.4	50.2	48.9	53.2
Easy	1,538	24.0	25.9	19.0	24.5	21.0
Living arrangements (*p* < .0001)						
No one	2,624	41.0	43.6	34.3	40.8	36.7
Spouse/partner	3,331	52.0	51.9	52.2	48.9	57.0
Own children	263	4.1	2.0	9.5	5.9	4.8
Other	186	2.9	2.5	3.9	4.4	1.5
Housing (*p* < .0001)						
House	4,884	76.3	70.0	89.4	86.9	81.0
Flat/unit/apartment	1,059	16.5	20.4	8.1	10.6	13.7
Retirement village	371	5.8	8.1	1.0	1.7	4.1
Other/mobile home/caravan	90	1.4	1.5	1.5	0.8	1.3
Area of residence (*p* < .0001)						
Urban	2,722	42.5	44.3	38.0	40.0	43.0
Large rural	751	11.7	11.8	10.6	11.5	15.2
Small rural	979	15.3	15.7	14.1	14.5	16.7
Other rural/remote	1,952	30.5	28.3	37.4	34.1	25.1

Table 2 presents estimates of mean levels of PF and MHI, adjusted for various sociodemographic variables, by companion animal status at Surveys 2 and 3. Although the differences *between* categories were only marginally significant ($p = .043$), post hoc comparisons revealed clear declines in PF from Survey 2 to Survey 3 ($p < .0001$ for all categories of companion animal status except other, for which $p = .035$). In contrast, all of the sociodemographic variables, except area of residence and moved house, were strongly associated with differences in PF ($p < .0001$). Companion animal status was not associated with differences in mental health scores at Surveys 2 or 3.

Table 3 presents the results of analyses examining associations between change in companion animal status and mean levels of PF and MHI across the two surveys. The differences in PF between categories of changed pet ownership (e.g., moving from owning no pet at Survey 2 to owning a pet at Survey 3) were marginal ($p = .09$) and small compared to the overall decline in physical functioning as a result of the passage of time. The declines in PF on post hoc comparisons of pairwise differences were significant ($p < .0001$) for all four categories of changed pet ownership. There were no significant differences in MHI associated with changes in companion animal status.

The question used in the ALSWH surveys only asked whether the women lived with a companion animal and not who was the primary caretaker of the animal. However, when data from women who lived alone (and therefore presumably did care for the animal) were analyzed separately, the results did not differ from the main findings reported. Similarly, given the purported effects of exercise on health and the role of dog ownership in increasing physical activity, women in the dog and cat categories were examined for differing effects on physical activity; however, no specific effects of dog or cat companion status were found.

The analyses were also conducted without adjustment for other demographic factors. The results did not differ much from the adjusted means shown in Tables 2 and 3, implying that effect modification is not a complete explanation for the lack of effects of pet ownership.

Discussion

Our analyses of the relations between living with a companion animal and mental and physical health appeared to be subject to the effects of demographics, both on associations with mental and physical health variables themselves and on the likelihood that a woman would be living with a companion animal at all. Women who live in family situations (not only with their spouse or partner), in houses (rather than apartments, retirement villages, or aged care facili-

Table 2. *Adjusted Means for Physical Functioning^a (PF Subscale of SF36) and Mental Health Index^b (MHI Subscale of SF36) by Categories of Living With a Companion Animal*

Companion Animal Status	PF ($p = .043$)		MHI ($p = .36$)	
	Survey 2	Survey 3	Survey 2	Survey 3
No pet	64.3 (63.6, 64.9)	59.3 (58.6, 59.9)	80.1 (79.7, 80.6)	79.6 (79.1, 80.0)
Dog	64.4 (63.3, 65.5)	58.6 (57.4, 59.7)	79.9 (79.2, 80.6)	79.1 (78.3, 79.8)
Cat	63.0 (61.4, 64.5)	58.8 (57.2, 60.4)	80.0 (79.0, 81.1)	78.6 (77.5, 79.7)
Other	61.9 (60.1, 63.7)	59.6 (57.7, 61.6)	79.0 (77.8, 80.3)	78.8 (77.5, 80.1)

^aPF model: Other variables in model and significance levels: manage on income ($p < .0001$), level of physical activity ($p < .0001$), housing ($p < .0001$), area of residence ($p = .09$), living arrangements ($p = .02$), moved house ($p = .11$) at Surveys 2 and 3.
^bMHI model: Other variables in model and significance levels: manage on income ($p < .0001$), level of physical activity ($p < .0001$), housing ($p = .01$), area of residence ($p = .01$), living arrangements ($p < .0001$), moved house ($p = .20$) at Surveys 2 and 3.

Table 3. *Adjusted Means for Physical Functioning^a (PF Subscale of SF36) and Mental Health Index^b (MHI Subscale of SF36) for Categories of Changes in Living With a Companion Animal Across Surveys*

	PF ($p = .09$)		MHI ($p = .14$)	
	Survey 2	Survey 3	Survey 2	Survey 3
No pet→no pet	64.0 (62.9, 65.1)	59.1 (58.0, 60.2)	79.7 (79.0, 80.4)	78.9 (78.2, 79.6)
Pet→pet	64.5 (63.8, 65.2)	59.5 (58.8, 60.3)	80.3 (79.9, 80.8)	79.8 (79.3, 80.2)
No pet→pet	61.6 (59.6, 63.6)	57.4 (55.3, 59.4)	79.6 (78.3, 80.9)	78.9 (77.6, 80.2)
Pet →no pet	62.0 (59.5, 64.5)	56.7 (56.2, 59.2)	78.6 (77.0, 80.2)	77.7 (76.1, 79.3)

^aPF model: Other variables in model and significance levels: manage on income ($p < .0001$), level of physical activity ($p < .0001$), housing ($p < .0001$), area of residence ($p = .07$), living arrangements ($p = .04$), moved house ($p = .13$) at Surveys 2 and 3.
^bMHI model: Other variables in model and significance levels: manage on income ($p < .0001$), level of physical activity ($p < .0001$), housing ($p = .009$), area of residence ($p = .08$), living arrangements ($p < .0001$), moved house ($p = .25$) at Surveys 2 and 3.

ties), and in country areas are much more likely to live with pets than other women. These demographic characteristics, as well as the women's ability to manage on their income, are strongly related to health outcomes.

Demographic and Other Factors

Pet ownership varies over the life course (Hart, 1993). Older women living with other people of different ages are more likely to have pets in their households. They may be living in these situations rather than independently (with or without spouse or partner) for a variety of reasons—for example, because their own health is failing or because they are assisting with childrearing. Therefore, they are likely to be a more heterogeneous group than women who live alone or only with their spouse.

Type of housing can affect opportunities for pet ownership (e.g., retirement village rules) as can living in rural areas compared to cities. However, these factors are also related to health. Health is generally poorer in rural areas. For example, a report by the Australian Institute of Health and Welfare (AIHW, 1998) showed the health of people living in rural and remote areas is poorer than that of people living in metropolitan areas. The health of women living in institutional settings is also lower than those living independently (American Geriatrics Society, 1993).

Other questions remain unanswered. For example, although healthier people are more likely to own an animal, the order of causation is uncertain (Siegel, 1990). Some researchers (e.g., Albert & Bulcroft, 1988) have suggested that pets may fulfill various roles and functions across the life span; such a developmental perspective could be important in interpreting human–pet interactions and possible benefits.

Strengths of the Study

The strengths inherent in the use of this longitudinal database include large sample size, heterogeneity of living conditions but not age, and the wide range of demographic and health variables included in the study. These features make it possible to see how strong the effects of demographics are on associations between living with companion animals and health outcomes. In addition, the nature of such a dataset facilitates the examination of data from both a cross-sectional as well as a longitudinal perspective.

Limitations of the Study

Limitations of this study include the fact that only one question on companion animals was asked, and no information on level of attachment to the animal(s) or

responsibility for the care and welfare of the animal(s) was obtained (Garrity et al., 1989; Ory & Goldberg, 1983). The extent of attachment to pets has received much interest in the recent literature, and with more methodologically sound pet attachment scales this issue can perhaps be explored.

Another possible benefit of living with companion animals is that they require care, which in turn may have positive effects on one's sense of control and self-efficacy; this has been put forward as a mechanism through which social relations affect health and well-being (Antonucci & Jackson, 1987). Particularly for older or frail individuals who perceive themselves as primarily receiving care rather than being able to provide it, such an opportunity to provide meaningful care may help redress imbalances in support exchanges (reciprocity) in their relationships (see Antonucci, 1985; Uehara, 1995 for discussions of support reciprocity across the life span). Responsibility for caring for animals was not, however, explicitly asked in the ALSWH surveys.

In addition, reasons for change in pet ownership (e.g., a move to an institutional setting) were not known but could provide insight into issues such as grief on the loss of a pet. Another limitation of this study is the narrow age range and single gender (women), which means that the findings may not generalize to other life stages and across genders.

Implications and Conclusions

Inconsistencies in the literature on the relation between companion animals and health may be explainable by a variety of factors, including differing amounts of information on the nature of the human–pet relationship, different samples, and different methodologies. Living arrangements, ability to manage on income, and other basic demographic variables relate strongly both to health and to opportunities for pet ownership. Major effects of these factors mean that it is unlikely that the impact of the companion animals on health can be answered from observational studies, even when large epidemiological datasets are used. Well-designed and evaluated experimental studies, wherein the majority of such variables can be held constant or at least somewhat controlled and in which details of the human–animal bond and any attendant positive and negative sequelae are obtained, are required to answer questions regarding specific benefits of pet ownership.

The major implication of this study, however, should directly inform such future studies. The *opportunity* to interact with animals and to own and care for pets is, in some measure, reliant on demographic factors that also influence health outcomes. Our finding supports work by other researchers (e.g., Ory &

Goldberg, 1983), who observed a complex interaction between sociodemographic factors, pet ownership, and happiness. To uncover specific and replicable health effects of the human–animal bond, it may be necessary to study more homogeneous samples to minimize the effects of other factors. Although this might limit the generalizability of findings, it would allow for more tailored and specific recommendations to maximize positive outcomes from human–pet relationships. This finding also points out the need for empirical studies that examine the effects of pet ownership *as a central research question* rather than as a peripheral finding. In this way, improved methodological rigor, such as random assignment to animal contact groups, would minimize the effects of demographic factors.

Positive psychology asks psychologists to focus on constructive human processes, emotions, and strengths (Sheldon & King, 2001). To be assured that we are indeed describing the mechanisms of such a potentially powerful positive relationship as the human–companion animal bond, we need to construct our study methods and analyses with care.

References

Albert, A., & Bulcroft, K. (1988). Pets, families, and the life course. *Journal of Marriage and the Family, 50*, 543–552.

Allen, K., Blascovitch, J., & Mendes, W. B. (2002). Cardiovascular reactivity and the presence of pets, friends, and spouses: The truth about cats and dogs. *Psychosomatic Medicine, 64*, 727–739.

Allen, K., Shykoff, B. E., & Izzo, J. L., Jr. (2001). Pet ownership, but not ACE inhibitor therapy, blunts home blood pressure responses to mental stress. *Hypertension, 38*, 815–820.

American Geriatrics Society. (1993). Older Women's Health (position paper). Retrieved March 28, 2004, from the American Geriatrics Society Web site: http://www.americangeriatrics.org/products/positionpapers/oldwmhlt.shtml

American Veterinary Medical Association. (1993). *US pet ownership and demographic sourcebook.* Shaumburg, IL: Center for Information Management.

Anderson, W. P., Reid, C. N., & Jennings, G. L. (1992). Pet ownership and risk factors for cardiovascular disease. *Medical Journal of Australia, 157*, 293–301.

Antonucci, T. C. (1985). Personal characteristics, social support and social behaviour. In R. H. Binstock & E. Shanas (Eds.), *Handbook of aging and the social sciences* (2nd ed., pp. 94–128). New York: Van Nostrand Reinhold.

Antonucci, T. C., & Jackson, J. S. (1987). Social support, interpersonal efficacy, and health: A life course perspective. In L. L. Carstensen & B. A. Edelstein (Eds.), *Handbook of clinical gerontology. Pergamon general psychology series* (Vol. 146, pp. 291–311). New York: Pergamon Press.

Arambasic, L., Kerestes, G., Kuterovac-Jagodic, G., & Vizek-Vidovic, V. (2000). The role of pet ownership as a possible buffer variable in traumatic experiences. *Studia Psychologica, 42*, 135–146.

Australian Institute of Health and Welfare (AIHW). (1998). *Health in rural and remote Australia.* Canberra, Australia: Author.

Bauman, A. E., Russell, S. J., Furber, S. E., & Dobson, A. J. (2001). The epidemiology of dog walking: An unmet need for human and canine health. *Medical Journal of Australia, 175*, 632–634.

Brown, W., Bryson L., Byles, J. E., Dobson, A. J., Lee, C., Mishra, G., & Scholfield, M. (1998). Women's Health Australia: Recruitment for a national longitudinal cohort study. *Women and Health, 28*, 23–40.

Bodsworth, W., & Coleman, G. J. (2001). Child-companion animal attachment bonds in single and two-parent families. *Anthrozoos, 14*, 216–223.

Eddy, T. J. (1996). RM and Beaux: Reductions in cardiac activity in response to a pet snake. *Journal of Nervous and Mental Disease, 184*, 573–575.

Friedmann, E., Katcher, A. H., Lynch, J. J., & Thomas, S. A. (1980). Animal companions and one-year survival of patients after discharge from a coronary care unit. *Public Health Reports, 95*, 307–312.

Friedmann, E., & Thomas, S. A. (1995). Pet ownership, social support, and one-year survival after acute myocardial infarction in the cardiac arrhythmia suppression trial (CAST). *American Journal of Cardiology, 76*, 1213–1217.

Garrity, T. F., & Stallones, L. (1998). Effects of pet contact on human well-being: Review of recent research. In C. C. Wilson & D. C. Turner (Eds.), *Companion animals in human health* (pp. 3–23). London: Sage.

Garrity, T. F., Stallones, L., Marx, M., & Johnson, T. P. (1989). Pet ownership and attachment as supportive factors in the health of the elderly. *Anthrozoos, 3*, 35–44.

Goldmeier, J. (1986). Pets or people: Another research note. *Gerontologist, 26*, 203–206.

Hart, L. (1993). Companion animals throughout the human life cycle: The contributions of Aline and Robert Kidd. *Anthrozoos, 4*, 148–153.

Kiel, C. (1998). Loneliness, stress, and human-animal attachment among older adults. In C. Wilson & D. Turner (Eds.), *Companion animals in human health* (pp. 123–134). Thousand Oaks, CA: Sage.

Lawton, M. P., Moss, M., & Moles. E. (1984). Pet ownership: A research note. *Gerontologist, 24*, 208–210.

Lee, C. (2001). *Women's Health Australia.* Brisbane: Australian Academic Press.

Lipp, O. V., Derakshan, N., Waters, A. M., & Logies, S. (2004). Snakes and cats in the flowerbed: Fast detection is not specific to pictures of fear-relevant animals. *Emotion, 4*, 233–250

McHarg, M., Baldock, C., Headey, B., & Robinson, A. (1995). *National People and Pets Survey.* Sydney, Australia: Urban Animal Management Coalition.

Melson, G. F. (1989). Studying children's attachment to their pets: A conceptual and methodological review. *Anthrozoos, 4*, 91–99.

Mishra, G. D., Ball, K., Dobson, A. J., Byles, J. E., & Warner-Smith, P. (2002). Which aspects of socio-economic status are related to health in mid-aged and older women? *International Journal of Behavioural Medicine, 9*, 263–285.

Netting, F. E., Wilson, C. C., & Fruge, C. (1988). Pet ownership and nonownership among elderly in Arizona. *Anthrozoos, 2*, 125–132.

Ory, M. G., & Goldberg, E. L. (1983). Pet possession and life satisfaction in elderly women. In A. H. Katcher & A. M. Beck (Eds.), *New perspectives on our lives with companion animals* (pp. 303–317). Philadelphia: University of Pennsylvania Press.

Parslow, R. A., & Jorm, A. F. (2003). Pet ownership and risk factors for cardiovascular disease: Another look. *Medical Journal of Australia, 179*, 466–468.

Raina, P., Walter-Toews, D., Bonnett, B., Woodward, C., & Abernathy, T. (1999). Influence of companion animals on the physical and psychological health of older people: An analysis of a one-year longitudinal study. *Journal of the American Geriatrics Society, 47,* 323–329.

Sable, P. (1995). Pets, attachment and well-being across the life cycle. *Social Work, 40,* 334–341.

SAS Institute. (1999). *SAS/STAT users guide* (version 8). Cary, NC: SAS Institute, Inc.

Serpell, J. (1991). Beneficial effects of pet ownership on some aspects of human health and behaviour. *Journal of the Royal Society of Medicine, 84,* 717–720.

Sheldon, K. M., & King, L. (2001). Why positive psychology is necessary. *American Psychologist, 56,* 216–217.

Siegel, J. M. (1990). Stressful life events and use of physician services among the elderly: The moderating role of pet ownership. *Journal of Personality and Social Psychology, 58,* 1081–1086.

Simons, L. A., McCallum, J., & Simons, J. (1997). Pet ownership and future health. *Medical Journal of Australia, 167,* 231–232.

Simons, L. A., Simons, J., McCallum, J., & Friedlander, Y. (2000). Pet ownership is not associated with future health: A nine year prospective study in older Australians. *Australasian Journal on Ageing, 19,* 139–142.

Stallones, L., Marx, M. B., Garrity, T. F., & Johnson, T. P. (1991). Pet ownership and attachment in relation to the health and US adults, 21 to 64 years of age. *Anthrozoos, 4,* 100–111.

Straede, C. M., & Gates, G. R. (1993). Psychological health in a population of Australian cat owners. *Anthrozoos, 6,* 30–42.

Uehara, E. S. (1995). Reciprocity reconsidered: Gouldner's "moral norm of reciprocity" and social support. *Journal of Social and Personal Relationships, 12,* 483–502.

Ware, J. E. (1999). SF–36 health survey. In M. E. Maruish (Ed.), *The use of psychological testing for treatment planning and outcomes assessment* (2nd ed., pp. 1227–1246). Mahwah, NJ: Lawrence Erlbaum Associates, Inc.

Ware, J. E., & Sherbourne, C. D. (1992). The MOS 36-item short-form health survey (SF–36): 1. Conceptual framework and item selection. *Medical Care, 30,* 473–483.

Wells, Y., & Rodi, H. (2000). Effects of pet ownership on the health and well-being of older people. *Australasian Journal on Ageing, 19,* 143–148.

Wilson, C. C., & Netting, F. E. (1987). New directions: Challenges for human- animal bond research and the elderly. *Journal of Applied Gerontology, 61,* 189–200.

Zasloff, R. L., & Kidd, A. H. (1994). Attachment to feline companions. *Psychological Reports, 74,* 747–752.

International Journal of Behavioral Medicine
2005, Vol. 12, No. 2, 111–122

Avoidance and Processing as Predictors of Symptom Change and Positive Growth in an Integrative Therapy for Depression

Adele M. Hayes, Christopher G. Beevers, Greg C. Feldman, Jean-Philippe
Laurenceau, and Carol Perlman

Depression is a leading cause of disability worldwide and can worsen the course of a variety of medical illnesses. There is a clear need to develop more potent treatments for this debilitating disorder and prevent its return. We are developing a promising psychotherapy that integrates components of current, empirically supported therapies for depression and also teaches healthy lifestyle and emotion regulation habits to promote psychological health. In the 1st open trial, growth curve analyses revealed a significant linear decrease in symptoms of depression in a sample of 29 clients who completed the therapy. Participants wrote essays about their depression each week, and the content was analyzed using a new coding system of change processes. Hierarchical linear modeling (HLM) revealed that peak levels of processing in the essays were associated with more improvement in depression and with the expression of more hope and of both negative and positive views of the self, presumably as clients explored their depressive views of self. Peak levels of avoidance were associated with less improvement in depression and with more hopelessness and negative views of the self. These preliminary results suggest possible targets of change that can facilitate symptom reduction and perhaps also promote psychological health.

Key words: depression, avoidance, rumination, emotion regulation, emotional processing, cognitive processing, expressive writing

The World Health Organization estimates that major depressive disorder is a leading cause of disability worldwide (Murray & Lopez, 1998). There is increasing evidence that depression is a recurrent disorder that often has a chronic course (Judd et al., 1998) and a serious risk of suicide (Bostwick & Pankratz, 2000). Major depression and even subsyndromal depressive symptoms are also associated with substantial physical health risks (Kiecolt-Glaser, McGuire, Robles, & Glaser, 2002). A special issue of *Biological Psychiatry*

recently reviewed research on the serious and adverse effects of mood disorders on a range of medical illnesses, such as cancer (Spiegel & Giese-Davis, 2003), cardiovascular disease (Carney & Freedland, 2003; Joynt, Whellan, & O'Connor, 2003; Kaufmann, 2003), HIV (Leserman, 2003), and diabetes (Musselman, Betan, Larsen, & Phillips, 2003). This comorbidity of depression and physical disease was declared a major public health problem and improving detection and treatment of depression a research priority (Evans & Charney, 2003; Stover, Fenton, Rosenfeld, & Insel, 2003). The articles in that series review evidence that depression can increase susceptibility to physical diseases, worsen their course, and increase risk of mortality. Katon (2003) also reviewed the adverse effects of depression on health habits, such as smoking, poor dietary habits, inactivity, and adherence to medical regimens.

Currently available treatments for unipolar depression have overall efficacy rates of 50% to 60%, and relapse rates are disturbingly high. A recent National Institute of Mental Health Psychosocial Intervention Development Workgroup called for the development of more effective interventions that address both symptom change and functional capacity, and they recommended the systematic study of the process of change to guide future treatment development (Hollon, Muñoz, et al.,

Adele M. Hayes, Department of Psychology, University of Delaware, Newark, DE 19716–2577, USA; Christopher G. Beevers, Department of Psychology, University of Texas at Austin, Austin, TX 78712, USA; Gregory C. Feldman and Jean-Philippe Laurenceau at the Department of Psychology, University of Miami, Coral Gables, FL 33146, USA; Carol Perlman, Department of Psychiatry, Massachusetts General Hospital, Boston, MA 02114, USA.

This project was supported in part by National Institute of Mental Health grant R21 MH62662 and by a University of Miami Provost Award to the first author. We thank William Galyardt, David Greenawalt, Melanie Harris, Jose Sandoval, Jamie Lewis Smith, Jennifer Strauss, Barbara Wolfsdorf, and our research and therapist teams. We also thank all of the participants in this study. This work was conducted in part when the first author was at the University of Miami.

Correspondence concerning this article should be addressed to Adele M. Hayes, Department of Psychology, University of Delaware, 108 Wolf Hall, Newark, DE, 19716–2577, USA. E-mail: ahayes@psych.udel.edu

2002). Given the comorbidity between depression and physiological functioning, improving depression treatment could have a substantial impact on a variety of health outcomes. We describe a therapy that we are developing to reduce the symptoms of depression and also promote psychological health. This therapy integrates components of existing empirically supported psychotherapies for depression to address the range of factors that influence the course of depression. It also involves teaching healthy lifestyle skills that can facilitate adjustment in the face of adversity. The interventions are organized around a framework of emotion regulation principles. This open trial was designed to examine the initial efficacy of this therapy and to allow for the study of change in symptoms, as well as variables associated with positive growth. We also describe a coding system that was used to study the weekly essays that clients wrote about their depression over the course of therapy. This coding system can be used to study change in psychotherapy, as well as adjustment to difficult life circumstances and chronic medical conditions.

Emotion Regulation and Mental Health

Several lines of research suggest that emotion regulation is an essential component of mental health and that problems of regulation are associated with a variety of forms of psychopathology (Cicchetti, Ackerman, & Izard, 1995; Davison, 2000; Gross, 1998). One way to regulate emotions is to avoid them. S. Hayes, Wilson, Gifford, Follette, and Strosahl (1996) describe a type of regulation called experiential avoidance, which includes avoidance of emotions, thoughts, images, memories, and physical sensations. They acknowledge that avoidance can at times be useful, but this strategy becomes problematic when it persists when costly, ineffective, or "life distorting." Avoidance of negative experiences can involve passive resignation, distraction, denial, cognitive distortion, suppression, repression, substance abuse, self-harm, disengagement, dissociation, and even suicide (Ottenbreit & Dobson, 2004).

Another problem of emotion regulation can involve getting preoccupied, consumed, or overtaken by emotions and experiences. It is important to know when it is no longer productive to engage. Overengagement can involve rumination, worry, obsessions, recurrent cravings and strong urges, and compulsive behavior. There is now substantial evidence that both avoidance and overengagement with emotions are associated with worse psychological and health outcomes (Gross, 2002; Kiecolt-Glaser et al., 2002; Salovey, Rothman, Detweiler, & Steward, 2000; Segerstrom, Stanton, Alden, & Shortridge, 2003).

Individuals prone to depression often engage in a process called rumination that involves dwelling repetitively and passively on one's negative mood and circumstances and on themes of hopeless, failure, incompetence, and worthlessness (Lyubomirsky & Nolen-Hokesema, 1993; Nolen-Hoeksema, 1991; Watkins & Baracaia, 2001). Rumination can extend the duration of depressed mood (Nolen-Hoeksema, 1991), predict the onset of symptoms of both depression and anxiety (Nolen-Hoeksema, 2000), and predict relapse (Segal, Williams, & Teasdale, 2002). Although there are other more productive types of rumination (Martin & Tesser, 1996), depressive rumination reflects an overengagement with emotions and thoughts.

The rumination process is easily activated and quickly becomes overwhelming. A common way to disengage from and prevent rumination is to try to avoid negative thoughts and emotions (Ottenbreit & Dobson, 2004; Segal et al., 2002). Unfortunately, there is some evidence that such avoidance is associated with a rebound and intrusion of the avoided material and the perpetuation of an avoidance-intrusion-rumination cycle (Beevers, Wenzlaff, Hayes, & Scott, 1999; Brewin, Reynolds, & Tata, 1999; Segal et al., 2002; Wenzlaff & Luxton, 2003). This pattern of vacillation between avoidance and rumination makes it difficult to experience and express emotions and to integrate and make meaning of experiences, a term called *processing.*

Brewin et al. (1999) reviewed evidence that as many as 73% to 87% of depressed individuals report a high frequency and prevalence of intrusive memories, thoughts, and feelings, which are similar to the rates of those with posttraumatic stress disorder (PTSD). They hypothesize that the avoidance-intrusion-rumination cycle in depression might be similar to that which occurs in PTSD and might reflect the presence of "unprocessed" experiences associated with depression. Avoidance can be associated with premature inhibition of processing and also with intrusion and chronic, unproductive processing, such as rumination (Brewin, Dalgleish, & Joseph, 1996; Reynolds & Brewin, 1999). From an experiential–humanistic perspective, Greenberg and colleagues also hypothesize that depression results, in part, from incomplete processing of emotional experience (Greenberg, Elliot, & Foerster, 1990, Greenberg & Paivio, 1997). A somewhat related idea is the hypothesis that worry, rumination, and other forms of overengagement might focus one's attention away from other negative emotions and material (e.g., Borkovec, 2002).

Thus, important tasks in treating depression are to reduce the patterns of avoidance and rumination and to facilitate processing. Therapeutic processing is different from rumination in that it involves approaching rather than avoiding difficult material, deliberately attempting to make meaning rather than being overtaken by intrusive and repetitive thinking, and experiencing a shift in perspective and emotional response rather than brooding and getting stuck in a repetitive and unproductive processing loop (Brewin et al., 1996; Hunt, 1998; Nolen-Hoeksema & Davis, 2004; Tedeschi & Calhoun, 2004). There is consistent evidence that processing involves approach, activation, and tolerance of emotional experience, together with exploration, reflection, and making sense of the experience (Greenberg, 2002a; Greenberg & Safran, 1987; Whelton, 2004).

Processing is hypothesized to be a central variable of change across theoretical orientations in psychotherapy, and exposure-based interventions are a potent way to facilitate shifts in perspectives and emotional responding (Brewin et al., 1996; Foa & Kozak, 1986; Greenberg, 2002a; Samoilov & Goldfried, 2000; Teasdale, 1999; Whelton, 2004). Similarly, processing has been proposed as one way that expressive writing tasks might have their beneficial effects on psychological and physical health (Hunt, 1998; Pennebaker, 1997; Pennebaker & Seagal, 1999; Sloan & Marx, 2004a, 2004b; Smyth, True, & Souto, 2001). Processing is also hypothesized to be a crucial component of a phenomenon called adversarial or posttraumatic growth, whereby some individuals can positively reinterpret, make meaning, or even find benefits in the face of adversity (Linley & Joseph, 2004; Tedeschi & Calhoun, 2004).

Exposure-based interventions have not yet been examined as a way to facilitate processing in depression, although there is substantial support for their efficacy in the treatment of anxiety disorders (Chambless & Ollendick, 2001). There is, however, initial support for Greenberg's (2002b) experiential, emotion-focused therapy for depression, which can be conceptualized as somewhat consistent with the principles of exposure in that it is designed to decrease avoidance and increase engagement with difficult emotions. Behavioral activation (BA) therapy (Martell, Addis, & Jacobson, 2001) also has empirical support, but it focuses more on decreasing behavioral avoidance than on exposing one to difficult internal experiences associated with avoidance and rumination. The goal in BA is not to facilitate processing but rather to decrease avoidance behaviors. The efficacy of these therapies for depression suggests that the principles of exposure might apply to the treatment of depression, as well as to the anxiety disorders. To put our integrative therapy in context, we briefly review currently available psychotherapies for depression.

Current Psychotherapies for Depression

Current, empirically supported psychotherapies for depression focus on changing negative beliefs (A. T. Beck, Rush, Shaw, & Emery, 1979; J. S. Beck, 1995), interpersonal functioning (Klerman, Weissman, Rounsaville, & Chevron, 1984; Weissman, Markowitz, & Klerman, 2000), behavioral avoidance and coping skills (Martell et al., 2001), and engagement with emo-

tions (Greenberg, 2002b). The Coping with Depression course (Lewinsohn, Hoberman, & Clarke, 1989) focuses on cognitions and increasing activities and interpersonal contacts. A more integrative approach, cognitive behavioral analysis system of psychotherapy (CBASP), blends cognitive, behavioral, interpersonal, and psychodynamic components and is designed to treat chronic depression (McCullough, 2000).

Two relapse prevention programs with promising empirical support are well-being therapy (Fava, Rafanelli, Grandi, Conti, & Belluardo, 1998) and mindfulness-based cognitive therapy for depression (Segal et al., 2002). Both are variants of cognitive therapy that are group-based and introduced after the symptoms of depression have remitted. Well-being therapy focuses on increasing beliefs and behaviors associated with positive affect and life satisfaction, applying Ryff and Singer's (1998) model of mental health. Mindfulness-based cognitive therapy (Segal et al., 2002) teaches mindfulness meditation as a way to learn to be aware of negative cognitions and emotions without becoming consumed by them. This process, referred to as "decentering," is hypothesized to decrease emotional reactivity, rumination, and the escalation of depressed mood.

In their comprehensive review of existing pharmacotherapies and psychotherapies for depression, Hollon, Thase, and Markowitz (2002) conclude that, although progress has been made, only about half of the clients who receive current treatments will respond, one third will meet criteria for remission, and of those who respond, many will relapse or experience a recurrence if they do not receive ongoing treatment. There is a consensus that treatment development is a high priority.

Current psychotherapies address different aspects of the cognitive, interpersonal, behavioral, and emotion regulation problems that maintain depression and increase the likelihood of its return; however, recent psychopathology models reveal that all of these problems influence the course of depression (e.g., Gotlib & Hammen, 2002; Riso & Klein, in press). One way to proceed in treatment development research is to combine components of existing empirically supported therapies for depression so that the range of variables that influence the course of depression are addressed (A. M. Hayes, Castonguay, & Goldfried, 1996; A. M. Hayes & Harris, 2000). Current therapies tend to focus primarily on one domain (e.g., cognitive therapy, interpersonal therapy, emotion-focused therapy, BA therapy).

In addition, current therapies focus on symptom reduction. Relapse prevention efforts often focus on maintaining treatment gains or on providing separate programs after recovery. Another approach is to teach skills and lifestyle habits that promote health, as part of the acute phase of treatment.

Another consideration in depression treatment development is to mobilize important processes of change that have been identified in research. As reviewed earlier, researchers in the areas of psychotherapy, stress and coping, and emotion regulation have identified avoidance and rumination as inhibitors of change and processing (using various labels for the construct) as a facilitator of change. Psychotherapy researchers have identified exposure as a potent technique for increasing approach behavior and facilitating processing. Therapies that directly target the avoidance-intrusion-rumination cycle and facilitate processing, while also teaching healthy lifestyle habits, might increase the long-term impact of treatments for depression. Such approaches could also be readily applied to medical populations.

The therapy that we are developing is designed to address the areas of vulnerability (cognitive, interpersonal, behavioral, emotion regulation) in depression and to teach skills in the acute phase of treatment that can be used beyond the depressive episode to increase resilience and promote mental health. The therapy actively targets avoidance and rumination, involves exposure to avoided material, and guides clients in processing difficult emotions and experiences. It also focuses on developing hope; healthy views of the self; and healthy lifestyle behaviors related to exercise, diet, sleep, and mindfulness meditation. Thus, this therapy integrates principles from the literature on psychopathology, the process of change, and wellness.

We present outcome data on the first open trial of this therapy and study the process of change to guide further treatment development. We examine processing and avoidance as predictors of change in depression. Clients wrote essays about their depression each week over the course of therapy. Change in avoidance, hopelessness, and a negative view of self were tracked over the course of therapy, as were health-promoting variables, such as processing of difficult emotions and experiences, hope, and positive view of self. Processing was hypothesized to be associated with change in depression, hope, and a positive sense of self. Avoidance was predicted to be associated with less processing and less change in depression, hope, and sense of self.

Method

Participants

All participants sought treatment for depression in a university-based community mental health center, and those who met criteria for major depressive disorder using the structured clinical interview for diagnosis (SCID; First, Spitzer, Gibbon, & Williams, 1995) were included in the study. Those who met criteria for bipolar disorder, psychotic disorder, borderline personality disorder, PTSD, obsessive-compulsive disorder, current substance abuse, or current suicidality were not included in the study and were instead referred back to the general clinic for treatment. The sample was 66% female and 34% male and was diverse in that 39% were White, 51% Hispanic/Latino, 2% Asian American, 2% African American, and 6% of other or mixed heritage. The mean age was 36.76 (range 16 to 58). Most participants had some college education (90%) and were not married or cohabiting (73%). The median number of previous depressive episodes was 2.5. Nine of the 33 participants (27%) had been taking antidepressant medication for at least 6 months prior to therapy and did not discontinue the medication during the therapy. Those receiving antidepressant medication tended to score somewhat lower on pretreatment depression scores on the Modified Hamilton Rating Scale for Depression Scores (MHRSD), $F(1, 31) = 3.65$, $p = .065$, but they did not differ significantly at posttreatment from those not receiving medication, $F(1, 31) = .23$, $p = .63$. Those taking medication also did not differ significantly from those who were not on medication on any of the other study variables.

Of the 33 participants who enrolled in therapy, 29 completed at least 12 of the 20 sessions of the program and were considered completers. Only four (12%) did not complete the therapy, and all of those discontinued before Session 8. Of the four who did not complete therapy, two clients moved, one became pregnant and had difficulty finding time for therapy sessions, and one discontinued for unknown reasons. Because we were interested in studying the role of processing, and the therapy is specifically designed to facilitate processing in the second phase of treatment, this study focuses on the completer sample.

Therapists

Therapists were 18 Master's-level doctoral students in clinical psychology, and two of the therapists were PhD-level therapists. Student therapists rotated through the Depression Treatment and Wellness Program as part of their practicum training. Therapists were 55% women and 45% men. Of these, 75% were White, 20% were Hispanic/Latino, and 5% were Asian American. Therapists received weekly individual and biweekly group supervision.

Depression Treatment and Wellness Promotion Program

This therapy is described in detail in A. M. Hayes and Harris (2000). The therapy consists of 24 sessions over the course of three phases. Throughout the entire course of therapy, clients are asked to write essays about their depression for 20 min each week. This task was designed to facilitate processing and also to assess the impact of sessions each week. Because there is consensus that current psychotherapies for depression may not be of adequate duration to prevent relapse, this approach includes more sessions in the acute phase and three monthly continuation sessions to help stabilize change. The therapy includes relapse prevention strategies in the acute phase of treatment. The skills taught in the therapy are designed to be used as part of a healthy lifestyle beyond the depressive episode.

The first phase of therapy (Sessions 1 to 8) focuses on *stress management*. This part of the therapy is designed to restore depleted energy, coping resources, and social support and to increase the motivation for change. Clients are taught problem-solving and coping skills, healthy lifestyle skills (e.g., healthy eating, sleep, and exercise habits), and mindfulness meditation. Clients are also taught about the consequences of avoidance and rumination as emotion regulation strategies. In addition, they are taught about healthy relationships and attachment patterns, and exercises are aimed at reducing interpersonal stressors, problematic patterns of interacting, and increasing social support. This phase includes psychoeducation, as well as exercises to initiate change. Because these healthy habits take awhile to incorporate into one's life, the skills are introduced early and addressed throughout the course of therapy and the continuation sessions.

The mindfulness mediation is introduced gradually and is conceptualized as a way to expose participants to the disturbing emotions and thoughts associated with their depression, without avoiding or ruminating. We teach mindfulness breathing exercises and the principles of decentering from disturbing thoughts and emotions so as to promote mindful engagement with internal experience, which can reduce emotional reactivity and increase clarity. This mindfulness component of this therapy applies principles from Segal et al.'s (2002) mindfulness-based cognitive therapy for depression relapse prevention program, except that we focus only on the mindfulness breathing exercises and apply the principles in the acute phase of treatment rather than only in the relapse prevention phase. Our initial research suggests that increases in mindfulness are associated with decreases in avoidance and rumination, which might prepare the person for the second half of therapy (A. M. Hayes & Feldman, 2004; Kumar, Feldman, & Hayes, 2004).

This first phase of therapy is similar to the 10-week cognitive-behavioral stress management program developed by Antoni and colleagues (Antoni, 2003; Ironson et al., 2002) except that our therapy is individual rather than group-based, and it is designed to target the problems of depression rather than adjustment to medical conditions, such as cancer and HIV and AIDS. The skills that promote adjustment, however, are similar. This phase of therapy is also similar to BA therapy for depression (Martell et al., 2001), except that the focus is more on broad-based health promotion behaviors rather than specifically on increasing approach behaviors.

The second phase of therapy (Sessions 9 to 18) is conceptualized as the *exposure* phase in that it involves directly activating and exploring the negative views of the future and the self, without engaging in avoidance and rumination processes. The skills and stability gained from the first phase are important and are brought to bear in this second phase of therapy. Clients write essays about their depression each week throughout the course of therapy. These essays not only track processing over time but also facilitate it. In the second phase of therapy, clients are asked to describe in session the negative view of self and hope that occurs when they are most depressed. They also reread the essays that they wrote about their depression in the early sessions of therapy. Clients then explore the historical antecedents of this negative view of self and hope. These exercises are designed to fully activate the depressive network of negative thoughts, affect, behavior, and even somatic responses. In this historical and affectively charged context, and without avoiding or ruminating, participants can begin to move toward processing difficult material and emotions and to formulate strategies to address problematic circumstances.

This approach is similar to exposure-based therapies for PTSD (Foa & Rothbaum, 1997; Resick & Schnicke, 1993) in that the person is exposed to avoided material without engaging in strategies to reduce the negative affect and instead is guided to process the difficult material. Our therapy involves less direct challenge of the depressive network than cognitive therapy for depression (A. T. Beck et al., 1979), and there is no work on identifying automatic thoughts and types of cognitive distortions. Instead, the therapy involves more guided exploration of the depressive material that is alternately avoided and mired in rumination. This exploration is more similar to schema-based cognitive therapies (A. T. Beck et al., 2004; Young, Klosko, & Weishaar, 2003) for personality disorders than to the original cognitive therapy for depression (A. T. Beck et al., 1979). Our therapy is also emotion-focused but differs from emotion-focused therapy for depression (Greenberg, 2002b) in that it is more directive and based on exposure models of therapy. Our integrative therapy also includes specific emotion regulation and mindfulness meditation exercises in the first half of therapy to reduce the symptoms of depression and to increase readiness for this more destabilizing second half of therapy.

The third phase of the therapy (Sessions 19 to 24) is the *consolidation and positive growth* phase. The depression has usually taken a toll on the person's interpersonal and occupational life, so we help people to move in a direction that is not based on working around the disability of depression. In this phase, we help clients to look to the future and set realistic goals for the upcoming months. We help them actively develop a more balanced view of the self that includes positive and negative characteristics, and we introduce exercises to clarify their sense of meaning and purpose. After depression, there is often a fear of hope, positive experiences, and viewing the self positively because of the potential disappointment that can follow. In a sense, the work in this phase involves learning to maintain steadiness in the face of both difficulties and positive experiences. We highlight again the importance of the life skills that clients have learned in therapy to regulate negative thoughts and emotions, and we review signs of relapse for that individual and relevant relapse prevention strategies that they can use.

There are three monthly *continuation* sessions designed to stabilize the changes made in the acute phase of therapy. In this phase, there is often vacillation between the depressive views of self and hope and the more positive views, which are not as well developed. The person will continue to experience life events, and the therapist helps the person to apply the life skills and principles learned to maintain the treatment gains and continue to develop these health-promoting habits. This phase focuses more on support than on initiating new change.

Symptoms of Depression

MHRSD. The MHRSD (Miller, Bishop, Norman, & Maddever, 1985) is a revised version of an interview-based assessment of depression severity that is a primary measure of outcome in most clinical trials of depression. The MHRSD contains 17 items that assess the same symptoms as the original Hamilton Rating Scale for Depression (HRSD; Hamilton, 1960), and the MHRSD also has acceptable reliability and validity (Miller et al., 1985). Ratings for these items are summed and typically used to determine depression severity.

The MHRSD was administered biweekly across the course of therapy. Because of the intensive assessment schedule, therapists administered the interview. An independent clinical assessor rated 20% of the sample of tapes for each client to assess interrater agreement on the MHRSD. Because total scores were used in all analyses, agreement was assessed on total scores. Agreement between raters was high (intraclass correlation = .92).

Process of Change

Essays. Following the methodology used by Pennebaker (1997) and recommended by Bolger, Davis, and Rafaeli (2003), clients were asked to write essays about their depression each week for 20 min. They were asked to write about their deepest thoughts and feelings related to their depression. These essays were designed to capture the impact of the therapy sessions over the week and also to facilitate processing over the course of therapy.

Coders. The coders were three doctoral-level clinical psychology graduate students and one bachelor's-level research assistant. Coders were trained to criterion for approximately 10 hr, with approximately 10 hr of practice coding. After reaching criterion agreement (intraclass correlation of at least = .80), coders rated the essays in pairs, and they were paired with each other coder an equal number of times. Weekly to biweekly meetings were held to review discrepancies and to prevent rater drift. Because agreement was good, the ratings of coders were averaged, and the averaged ratings were used in the analyses.

Coding of essays. The Change and Growth Experiences Scale (CHANGE; A. M. Hayes, Feldman, & Goldfried, in press) was used to code the content of the weekly essays. The CHANGE can be used to code the content of essays or of therapy sessions. The categories from the CHANGE that were coded in this study were avoidance, processing, positive and negative hope, and positive and negative view of self. Each item is rated on a scale of 0 (*not present or very low*), 1 (*low*), 2 (*medium*), and 3 (*high*). Categories can co-occur. For instance, it is not uncommon for essays to reflect ambivalence. One could write about both hopelessness and a glimmer of hope in the same essay.

Avoidance is defined as difficulty facing disturbing emotions, thoughts, or circumstances. Avoidance often involves attempts to block disturbing experiences and can include drinking or using other drugs to numb oneself, discontinuing the writing task because it is disturbing, avoiding therapeutic tasks, and isolating oneself from external stimulation (e.g., Level 3: "I can't stand myself any more. I need to shut my thoughts off. This weekend I sat home, drank, and listened to loud music. I can't write anymore about this stuff. It is making me sick.").

Processing is exploring and questioning issues and material related to depression, with some insight or perspective shift. Significant insight or a perspective shift often has emotional and behavioral manifestations. This category is designed to capture concepts that have been labeled as emotional processing (change in emotional information structures), meaning-making, benefit-finding, cognitive change, and schema change. Thus, it contains aspects of both cognitive and affective change. However, affective arousal without some insight or perspective shift is not considered processing. Rumination, worry, and other perseverative thoughts are also not considered processing. An example of Level 3 processing is

I have been through a lot. I realize that I have been spending so much time trying to run away from myself that I have lost my compass. I have ended up with a man who is not good for me and in a job that is below me. I put up with the hurt because I thought I did not deserve better. It had eroded my spirit. I felt like a dead person. That realization makes me feel nauseous and disgusted, but I am now discovering my strength and potential. It feels damn good. I had no idea what I was capable of. I am beginning to take chances again.

In this example, there is affective arousal, but the high level of processing is coded because of the significant insight and shift in perspective that also has affective manifestations.

Because we view positive hope and view of self as different from a reduction in their negative counterparts, we coded these categories separately. Positive hope and self are not coded if there is simply an absence of their negative counterparts; there must be evidence of positive descriptions that are at least somewhat elaborated. Positive hope is the extent to which the person describes an expectation that the future will be better and progress can be made on problem areas, as well as a commitment to change (e.g., Level 3: "I am beginning to see a way out of this black hole. I think I will make it."). Negative hope is the extent to which the person sees a disturbing and negative future, feels overwhelmed and stuck, sees few options, and has little motivation for change (e.g., Level 3: "Whatever…what's the point in trying? Things just keep piling up, and nothing I do makes any difference. Why do I bother?").

Positive self is the extent to which the person writes about the self as worthwhile, competent, deserving of respect, and otherwise acceptable. An example of Level 3 is

For the first time in a long time, I felt strong. I went to a community activism event and was myself. I felt so open and was able to connect with others again. I think I have something to offer to the group, with all that I have been through.

Negative self is the extent to which the person writes about feeling like a failure, incompetent, undesirable, inadequate, or otherwise flawed. An example of Level 3 is

Well, I sat around all day yesterday and thought about all the people I have let down. I was supposed to be the family success, and here I am sitting in a beat up, old rental barely able to hold down a slacker job. This is not how I imagined middle age. I have failed at everything I have touched. I'm the anti-Midas.

Interrater agreement on all coding categories was good to excellent (intraclass correlation = .73 to .84).

Results

Changes in symptoms of depression were examined in two ways. We report pretreatment to posttreatment change on the MHRSD, using t tests. Because we collected biweekly MHRSD scores, we also examined the trajectory of symptom change on all available data points, using individual growth curve modeling (HLM; HLM5, Raudenbush & Bryk, 2002). All regression coefficients presented from HLM analyses are unstandardized.

To study the process of change, we focused on two variables from the weekly essays, processing and avoidance, as predictors of the course of change in depression. An examination of the individual plots of these variables over the course of therapy revealed that both processing and avoidance scores tended to peak and then return to a low score. We, therefore, examined the peak (highest level) processing and peak avoidance scores in Phases I and II of therapy as Level 2 predictors of the trajectory of change in depression (MHRSD) across the course of therapy. This method of using peak values is often used in studies using the Experiencing Scale (Klein, Mathieu-Coughlan, & Keisler, 1986), a similar rating system that focuses on depth of processing. Gilboa-Schechtman and Foa (2001) also used this method in their analysis of peak levels of fear activation in recovery from trauma. Pretreatment depression severity did not significantly predict peak values of processing and avoidance in the first or second phase of therapy.

The plots of positive hope, negative hope, positive view of self, and negative view of self revealed more linear patterns of change, so we used the trajectories over the entire course of therapy in the analyses. Both peak processing and avoidance scores were examined as predictors of the trajectories of positive and negative hope and view of self.

Change in Depression

Depression (MHRSD) decreased significantly over the course of therapy in both the intent-to-treat and the completer sample, and the effect sizes were large (see Table 1). Treatment response was defined as a 50% reduction in symptom severity and no longer meeting SCID criteria for depression (Frank et al., 1991). Twenty-four (83%) of the completer sample ($n = 29$) responded to the therapy, two (7%) experienced a 36% reduction of symptoms, and three (10%) did not respond. The MHRSD was assessed biweekly, so we also examined the trajectory of change in the completer sample using individual growth curve analysis. There was a significant linear decrease in depression over the course of therapy ($B = -8.38$, $SE = 1.06$, $t = -7.90$, $df = 28$, $p < .001$).

Table 1. *Change in Depression on the Modified Hamilton Rating Scale for Depression (MHRSD) in the Intent-to-Treat and Completer Samples*

	Pretreatment		Midtreatment		Posttreatment		Pre to Post Difference	Effect Size (Cohen's *d*)
	M	**(SD)**	**M**	**(SD)**	**M**	**(SD)**		
Intent-to-treat (*n* = 33)	18.51	(5.84)	12.21	(7.06)	7.67	(5.74)	*t* = 8.47*	*d* = 1.87
Completers (*n* = 29)	19.41	(5.79)	12.28	(7.40)	7.10	(5.33)	*t* = 10.03*	*d* = 2.21

*p < .001.

The Process of Symptom Change and Positive Growth

Processing was hypothesized to be associated with change in depression. Because the exposure-based work was concentrated in the second phase of therapy, we examined whether peak processing scores in the second phase were higher than in the first phase. Peak processing in Phase II was indeed significantly higher than in Phase I, Phase I: $M = 1.14$, $SD = .17$; Phase II: $M = 2.09$, $SD = .19$: $t(28) = -4.26$, $p < .001$. Avoidance can occur at any time in therapy, so it was not expected to be higher in one phase than the other. Peak avoidance scores occurred about equally in both phases of therapy, Phase I: $M = 1.46$, $SD = .93$; Phase II: $M = 1.48$, $SD = .83$; $t(28) = -.10$, $p = .92$.

In the next set of analyses, we used HLM to examine peak processing and peak avoidance scores in Phases I and II of therapy as predictors of the trajectory of change in depression (MHRSD). In HLM, these peak scores are Level 2 (between-person) predictors because there is one score per person predicting the course of change in depression. Peak processing in Phase I of therapy was not significantly associated with improvement in depression ($B = -0.91$, $SE = 1.44$, $t = -0.64$, $df = 28$, $p = .53$), whereas peak processing in Phase II was ($B = -5.33$, $SE = 2.10$, $t = -2.50$, $df = 28$, $p = .02$). Peak avoidance scores in Phase I also were not significantly associated with change in depression ($B = 0.52$, $SE = 1.17$, $t = 0.44$, $df = 28$, $p = .66$), but peak avoidance in Phase II was associated with less improvement in depression ($B = 1.51$, $SE = 0.68$, $t = 2.21$, $df = 28$, $p = .04$).

Applying an approach similar to that used in Tang and DeRubeis's (1999) study of sudden gains (rapid improvements in symptoms) in therapies for depression, we examined whether depression scores changed significantly from the session before the Phase II peak processing (prepeak) to the session after (postpeak). The same approach was applied to the analyses of peak avoidance scores. If the peak value was zero, the depression scores at the beginning and end of the second phase of therapy were used. Depression levels in the sessions that preceded and followed the peak processing scores were significantly different (*M* prepeak depression = 12.63, *SD* = 9.09; *M* postpeak depression = 8.26, *SD* = 6.7, *t* = 3.27, *p* = .003). The mean decrease

in symptoms was 4.37 points (*SD* = 6.95). There was less change in depression in the sessions that preceded and followed the peak avoidance scores, and the difference was not statistically significant (*M* prepeak depression = 10.96, *SD* = 7.44; *M* postpeak depression = 11.36, *SD* = 8.75, *t* = −.32, *p* = .74). There was instead a slight increase in symptoms (Mean change = −.39, *SD* = 6.41). We also examined the correlations between the relevant prepeak depression scores and the subsequent peak processing and peak avoidance scores. The preceding depression scores were not significantly correlated with the subsequent processing scores, *r*(29) = .09, *p* = .63, or avoidance scores, *r*(29) = .18, *p* = .36. Together, these findings suggest that peak levels of processing and avoidance in the second of two phases were not simply a function of prior depression level.

HLM was then used to examine Phase II peak processing and avoidance scores as Level 2 predictors of the trajectories positive and negative hope and view of self (across sessions). Phase II peak processing levels were associated with significantly more statements of hope ($B = .43$, $SE = .05$, $t = 9.50$, $df = 28$, $p < .001$) and positive view of self ($B = .11$, $SE = .03$, $t = 4.11$, $df = 28$, $p < .001$), as well as statements reflecting a negative view of self ($B = .15$, $SE = .07$, $t = 2.33$, $df = 28$, $p = .028$). Peak processing in phase II was not significantly associated with statements of hopelessness ($B = .10$, $SE = .10$, $t = 0.99$, $df = 28$, $p = .33$). Phase II peak avoidance was specific to the negative statements in that it was associated with more hopelessness ($B = .34$, $SE = .14$, $t = 2.34$, $df = 28$, $p = .027$) and negative view of self ($B = .23$, $SE = .11$, $t = 2.01$, $df = 28$, $p = .05$) but was not significantly associated with positive hope ($B = .083$, $SE = .12$, $t = 0.66$, $df = 28$, $p = .51$) or positive view of self ($B = .009$, $SE = .04$, $t = 0.23$, $df = 28$, $p = .82$).

Discussion

Depression is a leading cause of disability worldwide (Murray & Lopez, 1997). It has serious health implications, and there is a need for treatment development, especially to address the problems of relapse and recurrence (Hollon, Muñoz et al., 2002). We are developing a promising psychotherapy that integrates components of current, empirically supported therapies for depression and strategies to promote wellness and to facilitate adjustment to difficult life circumstances. The efficacy data from this open trial are promising in that depression improved significantly, and we identified two important correlates of change in depression—peak levels of processing and avoidance.

Building on the literature on the process of change in therapy (Brewin et al., 1996; Foa & Kozak, 1986; Greenberg, 2002a; Samoilov & Goldfried, 2000; Teasdale, 1999; Whelton, 2004), expressive writing (Hunt, 1998; Pennebaker, 1997; Pennebaker & Seagal, 1999; Sloan & Marx, 2004a, 2004b; Smyth et al., 2001), and adversarial growth (Linley & Joseph, 2004; Tedeschi & Calhoun, 2004), we hypothesized that more processing would be associated with more symptom reduction. Peak processing scores were elevated in the second phase of therapy, when clients were taught to approach and explore the sense of hopelessness, defectiveness, and failure associated with their depression. This was done gradually and in a structured way so that this task would not degrade into rumination or avoidance. Peak processing scores during this exposure phase were associated with improvement in depression (MHRSD), both across the course of therapy and from the session before to the session after the peak scores. Prepeak depression scores did not predict the subsequent level of processing, which suggests that it was not only those who were less depressed who had higher levels of processing.

Peak processing was also associated with the expression of more hope and a positive view of self in the weekly essays. These findings are similar to recent work by Pos, Greenberg, Goldman, and Korman (2003), who found that higher levels of emotional processing in the later phase of experiential therapy predicted more change in depression at the end of treatment.

It is interesting that peak processing scores in the second phase of our therapy were also associated with the expression of a negative sense of self in the essays. It could be that therapeutic processing involves both the activation and exploration one's depressive view of the self and the emergence of a more positive sense of self. It is possible for a more positive sense of self, identity, and sense of purpose to emerge in the midst of distress and suffering, as can be the case in adversarial growth (Baumeister, 1991; Linley & Joseph, 2004; Tedeschi & Calhoun, 2004). We also discuss elsewhere the idea that a period of destabilization, in which old patterns are activated and new patterns are developing, can precede change in depression (A. M. Hayes & Harris, 2000; A. M. Hayes & Strauss, 1998).

Consistent with a large body of research on the psychological and health consequences of avoiding and suppressing emotions (Gross, 2002; Keicolt-Glaser et al., 2002; Salovey et al., 2000; Segerstrom et al., 2003),

peak avoidance scores during the exposure phase of therapy were associated with less change in depression and with more statements of hopelessness and negative view of self in the essays. Prepeak levels of depression did not significantly predict peak levels of avoidance, which suggests that those with higher levels of avoidance were not simply those who were more depressed. Avoidance was not associated with the emergence of hope and a positive view of self. Avoidance is likely to interfere with the exposure work and may further inhibit change because it can ironically promote the intrusion of unwanted material and rumination. This style is the opposite of what is required for processing, which involves exposure to the difficult material, without avoiding or ruminating, before there is a perspective shift or change in meaning. It might therefore be important to prepare clients for change by introducing stress management and emotion tolerance exercises, as we did in the first phase of therapy. Even with this preparation, some clients still avoided, and it will be important to identify predictors of this avoidance and also to understand what is being avoided.

Positive psychology emphasizes the importance of attending not only to symptom reduction but also to health promotion. By tracking both negative and positive hope and view of self over time, we could study how these variables were associated with processing and avoidance, variables that were associated with more and less change, respectively. Processing was associated with positive growth in one's sense of hope and self. In contrast, avoidance seemed to be specific to depressive views of the future and self. A more optimistic view and positive sense of self are important components of mental health (Ryff & Singer, 1998) and therefore might facilitate further positive experiences (Fredrickson, 2001) and prevent relapse. In addition, we teach healthy lifestyle skills that participants can use well beyond the depressive episode such as mood regulation strategies; mindfulness meditation; and healthy exercise, sleep, and dietary habits.

The real test of this therapy for depression will be in its ability to reduce the rates of relapse with this recurrent disorder. We are collecting these data now. It will also be important to include a control condition to clarify the changes due to the therapy. In the next phase of therapy development, we plan to include a comparison condition, such as BA therapy (Martell et al., 2001), which is also designed to facilitate approach behaviors but does not include a focus on interoceptive exposure or any cognitive interventions or focus on schema change. BA is similar to the stress management phase of our therapy. It will be intriguing to investigate whether processing occurs with BA and predicts the course of change in depression in a therapy that is not designed to facilitate this. The extent to which avoidance and positive growth (positive hope and view of self) occur can also be compared. Another important task is to examine the extent to which processing, avoidance, and positive growth occur in other therapies for depression. The CHANGE (A. M. Hayes et al., in press) coding system allows for the investigation of roles of these variables across interventions. Another aspect of this program of research is to identify client variables that predict processing and avoidance and to better understand what is happening in the sessions and client essays that seems to differentiate the course of change. These are goals of our ongoing work.

Although the focus of this report is on treatment development and the process of change, we have also introduced a new measure with which to code the process of change in essays or therapy sessions. The 20-min essays, which are similar to those used in expressive writing research (Pennebaker, 1997), are an efficient way to gather useful data over the course of therapy, and the CHANGE coding system (A. M. Hayes et al., in press) is a relatively simple way to code the content of this material. This system also can be combined with other coding systems that are based primarily on word counts, such as Pennebaker's Linguistic Inquiry and Word Count (LIWC; Pennebaker & Francis, 1996). The CHANGE system can add unique information in that it can account for metaphor, irony, negation, colloquialisms, and other linguistic devices that are difficult to capture with word counts.

The processing item of the CHANGE is similar to O'Cleirigh et al.'s (2003) measure of depth processing. That measure is used by raters to assess the extent to which the individual is working through and resolving a stressful experience. The depth-processing construct consists of four components: positive cognitive appraisal change, experiential involvement, self-esteem improvements, and adaptive coping strategies. Our measure of processing is more circumscribed in that it focuses specifically on processing (questioning, exploring, experiencing insight, perspective shifts, and new meanings and emotional responses). The processing and avoidance categories of the CHANGE are also conceptually similar to those used in psychotherapy research, such as the Assimilation of Problematic Experiences Scale (Stiles et al., 1990), Experiencing Scale (Klein et al., 1986), and the Narrative Processes Coding System (Angus, Levitt, & Hardtke, 1999). Our processing and avoidance categories are also derived from research on adversarial growth (Linley & Joseph, 2004; Tedeschi & Calhoun, 2004). The most important difference and benefit of the CHANGE is that it is designed to study the process of change and growth, and thus it includes a number of categories that can be combined to test models of change rather than single variables. Because coding with the CHANGE is relatively quick, multiple essays or sessions can be coded to allow for the study of trajectories of the variables over time. The peak levels can also be identified rather than

randomly coding sessions, as is often done in therapy process research.

Conclusions

We have presented a promising approach for the treatment of depression that integrates principles from emotion regulation research and existing empirically supported therapies for depression and stress management. We also applied the expressive writing methodology to increase the degree of resolution in the study of change. Not only does this methodology allow for the study of trajectories of change because of the weekly assessments, but also expressive writing might facilitate processing by having clients articulate their thoughts and feelings about their depression, as they also verbalize them in the sessions. Our coding instrument, the CHANGE (A. M. Hayes et al., in press), might be a useful tool in the study of change in essays and therapy sessions. Both the intervention and the coding instrument were designed in the spirit of positive psychology, in that they focus on both symptom change and health promotion.

References

Angus, L., Levitt, H., & Hardtke, K. (1999). The Narrative Processes Coding System: Research applications and implications for psychotherapy practice. *Journal of Clinical Psychology, 55,* 1255–1270.

Antoni, M. H. (2003). *Stress management intervention for women with breast cancer.* Washington, DC: American Psychological Association.

Baumeister, R. F. (1991). Suffering and unhappiness. *Meanings of life* (pp. 232–268). New York: Guilford.

Beck, A. T., Freeman, A., Davis, D. D., & Associates. (2004). *Cognitive therapy of personality disorders.* New York: Guilford.

Beck, A. T., Rush, A. J., Shaw, B. F., & Emery, G. (1979). *Cognitive therapy of depression.* New York: Wiley.

Beck, J. S. (1995). *Cognitive therapy: Basics and beyond.* New York: Guilford.

Beevers, C. G., Wenzlaff, R. M., Hayes, A. M., & Scott, W. D. (1999). Depression and the ironic effects of thought suppression: Therapeutic strategies for improving mental control. *Clinical Psychology: Science and Practice, 6,* 133–148.

Bolger, N., Davis, A., & Rafaeli, E. (2003). Diary methods: Capturing life as it is lived. *Annual Review of Psychology, 54,* 579–616.

Borkovec, T. D. (2002). Life in the future versus life in the present. *Clinical Psychology: Science and Practice, 9,* 76–80.

Bostwick, J. M., & Pankratz, V. S. (2000). Affective disorders and suicide risk: A reexamination. *American Journal of Psychiatry, 157,* 1925–1932.

Brewin, C. R., Dalgleish, T., & Joseph, S. (1996). A dual representation theory of posttraumatic stress disorder. *Psychological Review, 103,* 670–686.

Brewin, C. R., Reynolds, M., & Tata, P. (1999). Autobiographical memory processes and the course of depression. *Journal of Abnormal Psychology, 108,* 511–517.

Carney, R. M., & Freedland, K. E. (2003). Depression, mortality, and medical morbidity in patients with coronary heart disease *Biological Psychiatry, 54*, 241–247.

Chambless, D. L., & Ollendick, T. H. (2001). Empirically supported psychological interventions: Controversies and evidence. *Annual Review of Psychology, 52*, 685–716.

Cicchetti, D., Ackerman, B. P., & Izard, C. E. (1995). Emotions and emotion regulation in developmental psychopathology. *Development and Psychopathology, 7*, 1–10.

Davidson, R. J. (2000). Affective style, psychopathology, and resilience: Brain mechanisms and plasticity. *American Psychologist, 55*, 1196–1214.

Evans, D. L., & Charney, D. S. (2003). Mood disorders and medical illness: A major public health problem. *Biological Psychiatry, 54*, 177–180

Fava, G. A., Rafanelli, C., Grandi, S., Conti, S., & Belluardo, P. (1998). Prevention of recurrent depression with cognitive behavioral therapy. *Archives of General Psychiatry, 55*, 816–820.

First, M. B., Spitzer, R. L., Gibbon, M., & Williams, J. B. W. (1995). *User's guide for the Structured Clinical Interview for DSM-IV Axis I Disorders (SCID-I/P), (Version 2.0).* New York: Biometrics Research Department, New York State Psychiatric Institute.

Foa, E. B., & Kozak, M. J. (1986). Emotional processing of fear: Exposure to corrective information. *Psychological Bulletin, 99*, 20–35.

Frank, E., Prien, R. F., Jarrett, R. B., Keller, M. B., Kupfer, D. J., Lavori, P. W., Rush, A. J., & Weissman, M. M. (1991). Conceptualization and rationale for consensus definitions of terms in major depressive disorder—remission, recovery, relapse, and recurrence. *Archives of General Psychiatry, 48*, 851–855.

Fredrickson, B. L. (2001). The role of positive emotions in positive psychology: The broaden-and-build theory of positive emotions. *American Psychologist, 56*, 218–226.

Gilboa-Schechtman, E., & Foa, E. B. (2001). Patterns of recovery from trauma: The use of intraindividual analysis. *Journal of Abnormal Psychology, 11*, 392–400.

Gotlib, I. H., & Hammen, C. L. (2002). *Handbook of depression.* New York: Guilford.

Greenberg, L. S. (2002a). Integrating an emotion-focused approach to treatment in psychotherapy integration. *Journal of Psychotherapy Integration, 12*, 154–189.

Greenberg, L. S. (2002b). *Emotion-focused therapy: Coaching clients to work through feelings.* Washington, DC: American Psychological Association.

Greenberg, L. S., Elliott, R., & Foerster, F. (1990). Essential process in the psychotherapeutic treatment of depression. In D. McCann & N. Endler (Eds.), *Depression: Development in theory, research, and practice* (pp. 157–185). Toronto, Canada: Thompson.

Greenberg, L. S., & Paivio, S. (1997). *Working with emotion.* New York: Guilford.

Greenberg, L. S.,& Safran, J. D. (1987). *Emotion in psychotherapy: Affect, cognition, and the process of change.* New York: Guilford.

Gross, J. J. (1998). The emerging field of emotion regulation: An integrative review. *Review of General Psychology, 2*, 271—299.

Gross, J. J. (2002). Emotion regulation: Affective, cognitive, and social consequences. *Psychophysiology, 39*, 281–291.

Hamilton, M. (1960). Development of a rating scale for depression. *Journal of Neurology, Neurosurgery, and Psychiatry, 23*, 56–62.

Hayes, A. M., Castonguay, L. G., & Goldfried, M. R. (1996). The effectiveness of targeting the vulnerability factors of depression in cognitive therapy. *Journal of Consulting and Clinical Psychology, 64*, 623–627.

Hayes, A. M., & Feldman, G. (2004). Clarifying the construct of mindfulness in the context of emotion regulation and the process of change in therapy. *Clinical Psychology: Science and Practice, 11*, 255–262.

Hayes, A. M, Feldman, G. C., & Goldfried, M. R. (in press). From insight to processing: Two measures of therapeutic change. In L. G. Castonguay & C. Hill (Eds.), *Insight and change in psychotherapy* (pp. 00–00). Washington, DC: American Psychological Association.

Hayes, A. M., & Harris, M. S. (2000). The development of an integrative treatment for depression. In S. Johnson, A. M. Hayes, T. Field, N. Schneiderman, & P. McCabe (Eds.), *Stress, coping, and depression* (pp. 291–306). Mahwah, NJ: Lawrence Erlbaum Associates, Inc.

Hayes, A. M., & Strauss, J. L. (1998). Dynamic systems theory as a paradigm for the study of change in psychotherapy: An application to cognitive therapy for depression. *Journal of Consulting and Clinical Psychology, 66*, 939–947.

Hayes, S. C., Wilson, K. W., Gifford, E. V., Follette, V. M., & Strosahl, K. (1996). Emotional avoidance and behavioral disorders: A functional dimensional approach to diagnosis and treatment. *Journal of Consulting and Clinical Psychology, 64*, 1152–1168.

Hollon, S. D., Muñoz, R. F., Barlow, D, H., Beardslee, W. R., Bell, C. C., Bernal, G., Clarke, G. N., Franciosi, L., Kazdin, A. E., Kohn, L., Linehan, M. M., Markowitz, J. C., Miklowitz, D. J., Persons, J. B., Niederehe, G., & Sommers, D. (2002). Psychosocial intervention development for the prevention and treatment of depression: Promoting innovation and increasing access. *Biological Psychiatry, 52*, 610–630.

Hollon, S. D., Thase, M. E., & Markowitz, J. C. (2002). Treatment and prevention of depression. *Psychological Science in the Public Interest, 3*, 39–77.

Hunt, M. G. (1998). The only way out is through: Emotional processing and recovery after a depressing life event. *Behaviour Research and Therapy, 36*, 361–384.

Ironson, G., Antoni, M., Schneiderman, N., Chesney, M., O'Cleirigh, C., Balbin, E., Greenwood, D., Lutgendorf, S., LaPerriere, A., Klimas, N., & Fletcher, M. A. (2002). Coping: Interventions for optimal disease management in HIV. In M. Chesney & M. Antoni (Eds.), *Innovative approaches to health psychology: Prevention and treatment lessons from AIDS* (pp. 167–196). Washington, DC: American Psychological Association.

Joynt, K. E., Whellan, D. J., & O'Connor, C. M. (2003). Depression and cardiovascular disease: Mechanisms of interaction. *Biological Psychiatry, 54*, 248–261.

Judd, L. L., Akiskal, H. S., Maser, J. D., Zeller, P. H., Endicott, J., Coryell, W., Paulus, M. P., Kunovac, J. L., Leon, A. C., Mueller, T. I., Rice, J. A., & Keller, M. B. (1998). A prospective 12-year study of subsyndromal and syndromal depressive symptoms in unipolar major depressive disorders. *Archives of General Psychiatry, 55*, 694–700.

Katon, W. J. (2003). Clinical and health services relationships between major depression, depressive symptoms, and general medical illness. *Biological Psychiatry, 54*, 216–226.

Kaufmann, P. G. (2003). Depression in cardiovascular disease: Can the risk be reduced? *Biological Psychiatry, 54*, 187–190.

Kiecolt-Glaser, J. K., McGuire, L, Robles, T. F., & Glaser, R. (2002). Emotions, morbidity, and mortality: New perspectives from psychoneuroimmunology. *Annual Review of Psychology, 53*, 83–107.

Klein, M. H., Mathieu-Coughlan, P., & Kiesler, D. J. (1986). The Experiencing Scales. In L. S. Greenberg & W. M. Pinsof (Eds.), *The psychotherapeutic process: A research handbook.* (pp. 21–71). New York: Guilford.

Klerman, G. L., Weissman, M. M., Rounsaville, B. J., & Chevron, E. S. (1984). *Interpersonal psychotherapy of depression.* New York: Basic Books

Kumar, S. M., Feldman, G. C., & Hayes, A. M. (2004). *Change in mindfulness in an integrative therapy for depression.* Manuscript submitted for publication.

Leserman, J. (2003). HIV disease progression: Depression, stress, and possible mechanisms *Biological Psychiatry, 54*, 295–306.

Lewinsohn, P. M., Hoberman, H. M., & Clarke, G, N. (1989). The "Coping with Depression" course: Review and future directions. *Canadian Journal of Behavioral Science, 21,* 470–493.

Linley, P. A., & Joseph, S. (2004). Positive change following trauma and adversity: A review. *Journal of Traumatic Stress, 17,* 11–21.

Lyubomirsky, S., & Nolen-Hoeksema, S. (1993). Self-perpetuating properties of dysphoric rumination. *Journal of Personality and Social Psychology, 65,* 339–349.

Martell, C. R., Addis, M. E., & Jacobson, N. S. (2001). *Depression in context: Strategies for guided action.* New York: Norton.

Martin, L. T., & Tesser, A. (1996). Some ruminative thoughts. In R. S. Wyer Jr. (Ed.), *Ruminative thoughts* (pp. 1–47). Hillsdale, NJ: Lawrence Erlbaum Associates, Inc.

McCullough, J. P. (2000). *Treatment for chronic depression: Cognitive behavioral analysis system for psychotherapy (CBASP).* New York: Guilford.

Miller, I. W., Bishop, S. B., Norman, W. H., & Maddever, H. (1985). Modified Hamilton Rating Scale for Depression: Reliability and validity. *Psychiatry Research, 14,* 131–142.

Murray, C. J. L., & Lopez, A. D. (1997). Global mortality, disability, and the contribution of risk factors: Global Burden of Disease Study. *Lancet, 349,* 1436–1442.

Musselman, D. L., Betan, E., Larsen, H., & Phillips, L. S. (2003). Relationship of depression to diabetes types 1 and 2: Epidemiology, biology, and treatment. *Biological Psychiatry, 54,* 317–329.

Nolen-Hoeksema, S. (1991). Responses to depression and their effects on the duration of depressive episodes. *Journal of Abnormal Psychology, 100,* 569—582.

Nolen-Hoeksema, S. (2000). The role of rumination in depressive disorders and mixed anxiety/depressive symptoms. *Journal of Abnormal Psychology, 109,* 504–511.

Nolen-Hoeksema, S. & Davis, C. G. (2004). Theoretical and methodological issues in the assessment and interpretation of posttraumatic growth. *Psychological Inquiry, 15,* 60–64.

O'Cleirigh, C., Ironson, G., Antoni, M., Fletcher, M. A., McGuffey, L., Balbin, E., Schneiderman, N., & Solomon, G. (2003). Emotional expression and depth processing of trauma and their relation to long-term survival in patient with HIV/AIDS. *Journal of Psychosomatic Research, 54,* 225–235.

Ottenbreit, N. D., & Dobson, K. S. (2004). Avoidance and depression: The construction of the cognitive-behavioral avoidance scale. *Behaviour Research and Therapy, 42,* 293–313.

Pennebaker, J. W. (1997). Writing about emotional experiences as a therapeutic process. *Psychological Science, 8,* 162–166.

Pennebaker, J. W., & Francis, M. E. (1996). Cognitive, emotional, and language processes in disclosure. *Cognition and Emotion, 10,* 601–626.

Pennebaker, J. W., & Seagal, J. D. (1999). Forming a story: The health benefits of narrative. *Journal of Clinical Psychology, 55,* 1243–1254.

Pos, A. E., Greenberg, L. S, Goldman, R. N., & Korman, L. M. (2003). Emotional processing during experiential treatment of depression. *Journal of Consulting & Clinical Psychology, 71,* 1007–1016.

Raudenbush, S. W., & Bryk, A. S. (2002). *Hierarchical linear models: Applications and data analysis methods* (2nd ed.). Thousand Oaks, CA: Sage.

Reynolds, M., & Brewin, C. R. (1999). Intrusive memories in depression and post-traumatic stress disorder. *Behaviour Research and Therapy, 37,* 201–215.

Riso, L. P., Miyatake, R. K., & Thase, M. E. (2002). The search for determinants of chronic depression: A review of six factors. *Journal of Affective Disorders, 70,* 103–116.

Ryff, C. D., & Singer, B. (1998). The contours of positive human health. *Psychological Inquiry, 9,* 1–28.

Salovey, P., Rothman, A. J., Detweiler, J. B., & Steward, W. T. (2000). Emotional states and physical health. *American Psychologist, 55,* 110–121.

Samoilov, A., & Goldfried, M. R. (2000). Role of emotion in cognitive-behavior therapy. *Clinical Psychology: Science and Practice, 7,* 373–385.

Segal, Z. V., Williams, J. M. G., & Teasdale, J. D. (2002). *Mindfulness-based cognitive therapy for depression: A new approach to preventing relapse.* New York: Guildford.

Segerstrom, S. C., Stanton, A. L., Alden, L. E., & Shortridge, B. E. (2003). Multidimensional structure for repetitive thought: What's on your mind, and how, and how much? *Journal of Personality and Social Psychology, 85,* 909–921.

Sloan, D. M., & Marx, B. P. (2004a). A closer examination of the structured written disclosure procedure. *Journal of Consulting and Clinical Psychology, 72,* 165–175.

Sloan, D. M., & Marx, B. P. (2004b). Taking pen to hand: Evaluating theories underlying the written disclosure paradigm. *Clinical Psychology: Science and Practice, 11,* 121–137.

Smyth, J. M., True, N., & Souto, J. (2001). Effects of writing about traumatic experiences: The necessity for narrative restructuring. *Journal of Social and Clinical Psychology, 20,* 161–172.

Spiegel, D., & Giese-Davis, J. (2003). Depression and cancer: Mechanisms and disease progression. *Biological Psychiatry, 54,* 269–282.

Stiles, W. B., Elliott, R., Llewelyn, S. P., Firth-Cozens, J. A., Margison, F. R., Shapiro, D. A., & Hardy, G. (1990). Assimilation of problematic experiences by clients in psychotherapy. *Psychotherapy: Theory, Research, Practice, & Training, 27,* 411–420.

Stover, E., Fenton, W., Rosenfeld, A., & Insel, T. R. (2003). Depression and comorbid mental illness: The National Institute of Mental Health perspective. *Biological Psychiatry, 54,* 184–186.

Teasdale, J. D. (1999). Emotional processing, three modes of mind, and the prevention of relapse in depression. *Behaviour Research & Therapy, 37,* S53–S78.

Tedeschi, R. G., & Calhoun, L. G. (2004). Posttraumatic growth: Conceptual foundations and empirical evidence. *Psychological Inquiry, 15,* 1–18.

Watkins, E., & Baracaia, S. (2001). Why do people ruminate in dysphoric moods? *Personality and Individual Differences, 30,* 723–734.

Weissman, M. M., Markowitz, J. C., & Klerman. G. L. (2000). *Comprehensive guide to interpersonal psychotherapy.* New York: Basic Books.

Wenzlaff, R. M., & Luxton, D. D. (2003). The role of thought suppression in depressive rumination, *Cognitive Therapy and Research, 27,* 293–308.

Whelton, W. J. (2004). Emotional processes in psychotherapy: Evidence across therapeutic modalities. *Clinical Psychology and Psychotherapy, 11,* 58–71.

Young, J. E., Klosko, J. S., & Weishaar, M. E. (2003). *Schema therapy: A practitioner's guide.* New York: Guilford.

T - #0204 - 270225 - C0 - 280/208/4 - PB - 9780805894400 - Gloss Lamination